PLAY BETTER SQUASH

John Beddington

G2 entertainment

© John Beddington 2015

First published in 1974 by Queen Anne Press
Second edition 1977
Third edition 1984

This fourth edition published 2015 by
G2 Rights Limited, Unit 7-8 Whiffens Farm,
Clement Street, Hextable, Kent BR8 7PQ

*Front Cover photo of photo of Nick Matthew and James Willstrop
by Steve Line/SquashPics.com*

Back cover photo by Steve McFarland

ISBN 978-1-78281-236-4

CONTENTS

Foreword by Don Goodwin

My first exposure to John Beddington as an expert in the sport of Squash came in the early 80s. In 1983 in New York City he introduced me to the Loews Cup, an international team competition between Canada, the United States and Mexico. John produced the event from 1983 to 1990. The teams featured some of the leading lights in North American professional Squash at that time: Canada's Clive Caldwell, Mark Talbott and John Nimick of the USA and Mario Sanchez from Mexico. Everything about the event was first-class .... something I

learned was the trademark of anything done by John Beddington!

John's Squash career began when one of the biggest names in the sport was Jonah Barrington. I never had the pleasure of watching Barrington compete, but have had the honour of seeing the great Jahangir Khan, then Jansher Khan ... then through the Talbott years to Peter Nicol and Jonathan Power ... then to the great Egyptians Amr Shabana and Ramy Ashour. They all testify to the continuing broad international reach of this great game.

A useful club player himself, John first made his mark internationally as a squash club owner in the UK and Germany and, later, Canada. He managed top players and also served as consultant to the Squash Rackets Association (now England Squash), Squash Canada, and the Professional Squash Association among others. He created the first co-ordinated global squash circuit—the World Series of Squash in 1977 and was described in the late 70s by the Singapore Times as 'The Most Powerful Man in Squash.' He served as Chairman of the Canadian Open (softball) Squash Championships from 1985 to 1995 and was also Chairman of the British Open Squash Championships in 2003 and 2004.

And now Squash may yet be a part of the greatest showcase of all: the 2020 Olympic Games. No doubt the world-wide popularity of the sport will enjoy yet further growth as excitement builds and interest intensifies. So the time is clearly right for a book that captures all that is great about Squash and aims to guide not only the newcomer, but also those looking to take their game to the next level. How right it is that this golden treasure .... Play Better Squash by John Beddington .... should be re-published for the modern era in the form of an e-book (as well as in paperback), easily accessible to players the world over.

Some may know John for his truly extensive contributions to international tennis. A respected player himself, he has been involved with over 150 significant tennis tournaments in over 15 countries since tennis went 'Open' in 1968. He was Executive Vice President of Tennis Canada for 17 years and Tournament Director and Chairman of both the men's and women's Canadian Opens in Toronto and Montreal, ultimately being inducted into the Canadian Tennis Hall of Fame in 2006. He founded the highly respected Masters Tennis at the Royal Albert Hall in London now in its 18th year. He is a member of the All England Lawn Tennis Club at Wimbledon.

Things stand the test of time when they're done excellently the first time. John Beddington has always known only one way to do anything, that being absolutely first-class—with no shortcuts and no compromises. Play Better Squash was a classic as soon as it was first published, becoming a best seller, and should now be the ideal reference book for a new generation of players in its completely updated and revised edition.

It has been my privilege to observe John's handywork from the best seat in the house, functioning as master of ceremonies for Tennis and for Squash for 35 years, and for the 1996 Olympic Games. His insistence on excellence down to the smallest detail is an inspiration to all who work alongside him.

From this vantage point, it's a great pleasure to recommend to you Play Better Squash in this new edition. Squash is known for its many fitness benefits as well as the thrills and challenges it produces for its millions of participants. May this book help you bring all those wonderful benefits into your life for years to come.

"Safe Home"...
Don Goodwin
Sports Broadcaster and "Hall of Fame Master of Ceremonies"

Foreword to the First Edition

By Rex Bellamy, former Tennis and Squash Correspondent of *The Times* and author of books on tennis, squash and hill climbing.

A long association with tennis and squash has, among other advantages, granted me the privilege and pleasure of a close acquaintance with three congenial JBs: John Barrett in tennis, Jonah Barrington in squash, and John Beddington in both. All are energetically imaginative and have a rare capacity for opening windows in the mind. John Beddington, the author of this popular book, is the least well known of the three because his talents have primarily been exercised on the periphery of the courts rather than in the spotlight of personal publicity. But his relatively modest status as a player is, in this case, a recommendation; because he is writing mainly for his would-be peers in the higher echelons of club squash, for those who are facing, or are about to face, the kind of challenges he has met and mastered himself.

He was never taught squash, but picked up the game at Eton and subsequently reached a high level as a club player. That is probably more than most of his readers will achieve. But it represents a standard to which all can reasonably aspire if they have the ambition, ability, and character. This book helps them on the way because it is written by a man who understands their problems and is still young enough to share them. During the past I have played the author not only at his own club (a relaxed rendezvous for players at every level) but also, by a bizarre combination of circumstances, in Manhattan and at Salem in Massachussetts. His experience of American squash indicates an unquenchable enthusiasm for the game, no matter where or how it may be played.

His wide-ranging interests made him a director of the Lambton Squash Club in London, and the Top Squash Club in Frankfurt as well as European Tennis Director for the Grand Prix circuit and its climactic Masters tournament. He created and organised the World Series of Squash, the first coordinated international circuit of squash tournaments. He is recognised as one of the foremost Tennis and Squash Tournament Directors in the world. That in the midst of all this he found time to write an admirable and successful book on squash is at once remarkable and typical.

The bulk of this volume concerns tactics and technique. But there is also much solid information and sensible comment on wide areas of the game. The author is always good company and his readers benefit from the advice of a kindred spirit. They may also find future comfort in the fact that, if there are no squash courts in the next world, John Beddington is the kind of man who will build some.

Acknowledgements

There are many people whom I would like to acknowledge with reference to this book. Inevitably they cannot all be mentioned.

Knowledge gained in any subject, especially in a sport such as squash, is the result of many years experience, both on and off the court—mine is no exception. I have been lucky enough to meet and observe many people interested in the game including the world's top players, administrators and a number of enthusiasts. Most of these friends and acquaintances have contributed to this book, however indirectly, for my knowledge and enthusiasm for this superb game have been increased by contact with them.

When I first wrote this book over 40 years ago, I received considerable advice from my wife Roseann, who did not then, and does not now, play squash but who patiently and laboriously typed the manuscript on an old typewriter, before the days of computers or even word processors, and improved it in the process.

This version has been updated to reflect the changes the sport has experienced since it was last published some 30 years ago. The sport has improved and has certainly stood the test of time; it is a marvellous sport both to play and to watch.

I would particularly like to thank Richard Eaton and Ian Robinson for their help in revising the text for this edition; their input has been invaluable.

There are a handful of others whose support and encouragement over the years I would wish to acknowledge here: Mark Vere Nicoll and Colin White, my partners at Lambton Squash Club in the 70s; the late Mark McCormack, the founder of IMG, Andrew Shelley of the World Squash Federation, Jonah Barrington, Steven Jedlicki in Frankfurt, Clive Caldwell, Jane Wynne and Howard Seto in Toronto, Sylvie Asselin in Los Angeles, John Nimick in Boston, Sales Woody in Detroit and Chris O'Donoghue in London.

No acknowledgement would be complete without referring to the players who are too numerous to mention here.

Finally, I thank Rex Bellamy who used to write so fluently for The Times on both tennis and squash for his original foreword, and the irreplaceable Don Goodwin for the foreword to this new edition.

Introduction

So you want to play squash? Well, this book has been written not only for the beginner learning to play for the first time, but also for the player who has been hitting the ball around for some time and wants to improve his or her present standard.

For the beginner the first view of a squash court may seem daunting—a more or less square, gleaming pit with wooden floor, white walls and ceiling, no windows, and apparently no door. Many squash courts have glass back walls although when this book was first written forty years ago this was not the case. The first sight of squash being played may, of course, be equally disconcerting— two players running wildly to and fro whacking a little black ball around the walls with alarming enthusiasm.

However, the beginner can quickly appreciate the enjoyment to be gained from the game. The physical activity, the need for fast reflexes, and the concentration and anticipation make squash a superb fun and exercise game. For the more advanced player, improvement will bring ample opportunity for tournament and championship play at all levels, from club ladders and leagues to international status.

It has been said that becoming a champion is, like genius, the result of 90 per cent perspiration and 10 per cent inspiration. Squash is a game that exercises both the mind and the body, so that any effort to improve needs to be both mental and physical. However, to become a real champion at the game, the perspiration will be more of the mind than the body. Physical fitness is vital, but it is a small matter by comparison with the mental effort the average player must make for consistent improvement.

The popularity of squash has been maintained for many years, largely because it is a game suitable for both men and women of all ages—from those still at school to those approaching, or even well into, middle-age. It is also one of the most cosmopolitan games of our time.

Traditionally, books on sport are written by experts, for example, John McEnroe on tennis, or Tiger Woods on golf. This book is about squash—what the game is and how it is played. Above all, it is a game to be played with enthusiasm—and in that respect this book is written by an expert. Although there are countless squash players who are better than I ever was, there are few who take more pleasure in the game.

No other sport I know has the ability to provide such excellent exercise leaving one physically tested to the extreme, but with the added euphoria of leaving one with a totally clear mind.

Part One

1 SO YOU WANT TO PLAY SQUASH?

It had taken a lot of persuading. After all, James had not taken any form of exercise for three years and it had begun to show. His muscles, once proud and taut, were in an early stage of flabbiness and his waistline was not quite what it used to be. Not quite a paunch—he was only 28—but perhaps his friends were right. Squash might be the answer for him. It seemed to be popular with many people.

James's real problem was not fear of fierce exercise but fear of being ineffectual, which would severely damage his pride. In his earlier years he had kept quite fit and managed to be fairly competent at athletic games, but he would be a complete beginner at squash. Some of his friends at the office had played for years and their enthusiasm, to say nothing of their apparent fitness, was daunting. He did not particularly relish the thought of losing to any of them.

But the fight had been won. One cold winter's evening James found himself setting off for his first game of squash. He had found an old pair of trainers, a sports shirt and some football shorts that were a bit tight around the waist, and he was off, both nervous and excited, yet at the same time pleased that he had finally made the effort.

The squash club was pleasant and comfortable and his opponent greeted him cheerfully, with no hint of embarrassment at the strange assortment of sports gear that appeared from James's bag. James was not completely ignorant of the game—he remembered that it wasn't very different from tennis in some ways. One player serves, the other player returns, and the rally continues until one of the players makes a mistake. Instead of being on opposite sides of the court, squash opponents must share the same confined space, and instead of hitting the ball "over the net" it must be hit above a line on the front wall of the court. Squash couldn't be too difficult as it therefore consists of hitting a ball around in a four-walled room. Shots must be easier to make, as it is quite difficult to hit a ball out of a four-walled room—in tennis it is easy to send it too far or too wide.

James's opponent kindly lent him a squash racket, and he soon found himself on court about to begin the knock-up. His friendly opponent had chosen a very slow ball and James was somewhat taken aback to find that it hardly bounced at all—it merely plopped against the wall and refused to return to the back of the court. But

James was quick to learn that the ball must be warmed up, and that the best way to do this is to hit it as hard as possible at the front wall. So, with a swing of the racket and on flat feet, James began. He was pleasantly surprised at how simple it seemed to hit the ball at the wall, and, having realised that the wall is a vast area offering a great margin for error, he began to find squash less frightening. However, he had already begun to make mistakes that would be harder to rectify the longer they persisted.

James soon found that being able to hit the ball, he could begin to play a game. A quick discussion of the basic rules and the determination of someone who hates to lose soon enabled him to perform with reasonable competence. At the beginning, the pace of his improvement was his greatest encouragement, but after a while, although his enthusiasm remained and the will to practise strengthened, nothing more was achieved in terms of progress. It was at this point that James realised that he had improved as much as possible on his erratic beginning to the game and if he was going to improve any further he would need help. Furthermore, he was going to have to unlearn some of the faulty techniques he had developed.

Where could he go for help? Coaching is available from several sources, but it is sometimes expensive and inaccessible. However, a few books exist on the basic technical approach to the game — and this is another one! The idea that a book can teach anyone to play a game is debatable, but many fine sportsmen and women as well as ordinary club players use books and articles, as well as ebooks and other sources available through modern technology, to learn more about their own sport.

Squash is one of the games which most obviously can be learned from a book. It is not a difficult sport to begin, as James discovered, and there seems little reason why it should be a difficult sport to learn *correctly* once one has begun. Simple instructional passages on the basic strokes can be easily followed and put into practice.

Looking at the state of another popular game, golf; one beginner seeking professional advice on how to take it up was told to find a "basic swing", and then practise for six months before venturing on to the course. There is much to be said for this type of advice if the player in question has the determination of an Olympic athlete. Unfortunately most beginners have not, and so this book is not aimed at Olympic athlete types. The desire to improve is tempered by an eagerness to play matches. To be locked on a squash court for six months until one can hit the ball with unerring efficiency is perhaps the quickest way to improve, but it is certainly not the most enjoyable.

Play Better Squash aims to help the beginner, whatever his ambitions, to play properly right from the start. He can still play matches and it is hoped that he will; but if he follows the instructional sections, he will adopt the correct techniques and tactics in a simple progression, until he finds to his great surprise that he is playing good squash. That is not to say that poor James has been left in an anguished plight. The book will show him his errors, and on the strength of his own ability he will be able to rebuild a sound platform from which to improve.

That is what learning a new game means—the building of a sound technique that will not falter whatever the stresses and pressures applied to it. Allied to this comes a basic understanding of what can be achieved and of what the player is trying to achieve, whether during a particularly close game or during his career as a whole. It is hoped that this book will be of value not only to the beginner or to the moderate player; for if by its very simplicity it reminds the better player of some of the fundamentals of the game of squash, then it will be of help to him also.

The Game of Squash

The game of singles in squash is played between two players. One player serves the ball from one of the two service boxes on to the front wall above the service line and below the front wall line, so that it rebounds into the opposite back quarter of the court behind the short line and on the other side of the half court line. The server is known as *hand in* and the receiver is known as *hand out*. The right to serve at the beginning of a game is decided by the spin of a racket.

After the server (hand in) has served, the receiver (hand out) can return the ball by hitting it after it has bounced on the floor, or on the volley before it bounces. Whichever option he chooses, the ball must be returned, without bouncing on the floor either directly or by way of one of the other walls, to the front wall above the board or tin.

From that point, players hit the ball alternately and play continues until one of them fails to make a good return. This can happen if he does not reach the ball before it bounces on the floor for the second time, or if he hits the ball below the board into the tin or above the out of court line on any of the four walls. It is also possible to lose a point by standing in the path of an opponent's ball if it would have travelled directly to the front wall after he has hit it.

If a player has been hand in and loses a rally, he loses the right to serve and the hand out receiver becomes hand in as server. Points are won or lost at the end of each rally but the serve changes hands if one loses the rally.

The first player to reach 11 points wins the game unless the score reaches 10 all. If this happens the game is decided by 2 clear points. Matches are usually the best of five games, the winner being the player who is first to win three games.

This is a brief summary of how squash is played and the further you read the more you will understand. A beginner will soon notice the attractions of the game: plenty of exercise in a short period and

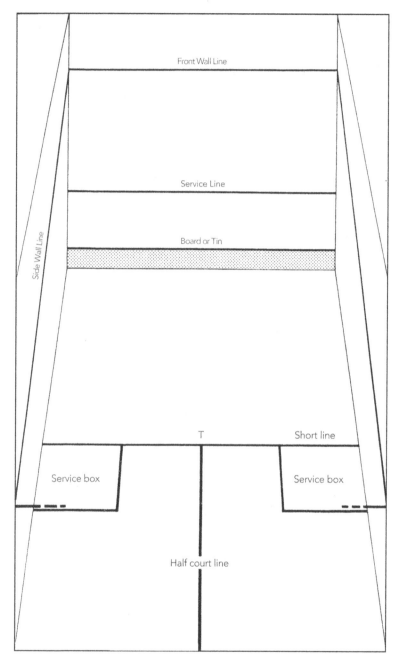

Front Wall Line

Side Wall Line

Service Line

Board or Tin

T   Short line

Service box   Service box

Half court line

Diagram 1   The court: definitions.

14

in a fairly limited area; unlike tennis or badminton, the margin of error in hitting the ball out of court is considerable—it is therefore easier to keep the rally going and requires less basic skill to be able to play at all; squash can be practised on your own without the absolute necessity of a partner or opponent (improvement in technique is also more likely to follow from practising alone); squash is invigorating.

Squash does not damage your ability or skill in other sports such as tennis. In fact it can enhance it. There are several very good tennis players and other sports celebrities who are also more than just proficient at squash. They use squash as a training ground for other sports since it requires sharp reflexes, breathing, speed, accuracy, and coordination.

Now let us move on to the technical requirements of the game.

Equipment and Clothing
Apart from the basic necessity of a court in which to play, the equipment and clothing required for playing squash can be readily obtained at any reasonable sports, or club professional's shop. Finding a court is easily achieved by searching the internet.

The basic equipment for squash is a racket and ball; the basic clothing includes shirt, shorts, socks, and shoes. Women can replace the shirt and shorts with a dress suitable for sport or a skirt and top. These items need not be expensive and you may find that you already have some of them if you play tennis.

The Racket
The choice of a racket depends on the individual, who must first decide upon the price range he can afford. Racket prices vary enormously, but for the beginner a modestly-priced one is quite sufficient.

The important point to remember about choosing a racket is that it should feel comfortable—the weight and the balance must suit the individual. The grip on the handle is also a matter of personal choice, and there are different materials to choose from. There are also a wide variety of strings available for your racket. It may suit you to begin with an inexpensive synthetic string while you are learning.

If you are reaching a level at which you are called upon to play a match then it probably makes sense for you to acquire a matching pair of rackets in case of breakage of frame or string. One other point to remember; however good or expensive a racket is, it will not last any longer than any other if it is hit hard enough against the walls or the floor.

The Ball
The ball and the racket are both defined in the final section of this book.

There are several types of what is basically the same ball—blue dot, red dot, orange dot, green dot, white dot or single yellow dot; and the double yellow dot ball which is widely used for all competitive play.

The speed of the ball varies not only because of its own specification but the type of court used. On a hot court the air inside the ball warms up with the result that the ball moves off the walls faster. Therefore, it is obviously better to use a slow ball on a fast or hot court, and a faster ball on a slow or cold court. Apart from using the type of ball most suitable for the court on which you are playing, it is generally easier for the beginner to start with a fast or blue dot ball.

Shoes
There are many varieties of shoe that can be used for squash, but a basic squash shoe with a good gripping sole is quite satisfactory as long as it is strong enough to cope with the pressures put on it by constant twisting and turning. The shoe must not have black soles which will mark the court's surface.

When buying shoes, bear in mind the thickness and number of pairs of socks you will wear.

Socks
It is most important that your feet feel comfortable when you are wearing socks and shoes, otherwise you will not be able to concentrate on your game.

Some players wear two pairs but most players find that one pair is sufficient. However many pairs you wear depends on your individual comfort. If your feet blister easily you may prefer to wear two pairs, though usually one thick pair is enough.

Always wear a clean pair of socks each time you play; apart from anything else, dirty socks cause blisters more easily. Look after your feet—wash and dry them carefully after playing; and use foot powder if you feel it necessary.

Shirts, Shorts, Skirts, Dresses etc
These clothes should be easily washable, and, most important, comfortable. They should not be too tight or too loose, or restricting in any way.

Other Equipment
Other useful items for the squash player include a towel, which is essential and should be available outside the court for use between games. Sweatbands and headbands can also be useful for the player who sweats heavily.

Eye guards are mandatory for juniors and recommended for all players due to the dangerous nature of eye injuries which can occasionally be caused by squash balls.

A wide variety of sports bags are available in which to carry your clothing and equipment.

Much of what has been said may seem obvious. However, it is necessary to stress the importance of these aspects of the game and also how preferable it is to have your own. Keep it in good condition and turn up on court looking well prepared in clean clothes. The advantage in doing so may be psychological—but it will be an advantage nevertheless.

The Court

The standard dimensions of a squash court are defined in the last section of this book. However, there are still some courts that have not been built to the standard international dimensions. These are either relics of the time when there was no standard specification for a court, or those which have been converted from other uses.

A court is basically 32 feet from the back wall to the front wall and 21 feet across. The diagram at the back of this book shows the dimensions. The walls of the court should be white and constructed of a special type of hard plaster which has to contend with considerable wear and tear. Most courts now have spectator facilities; some have glass back walls with a few rows of seats and others have galleries above the top of the back wall while a few have the capacity for spectators along the top of three or all four walls.

The floor should be well sprung and ideally made of maple, but other strong timber, such as pine or birch, may be used. However, the floor must not be treated with too much seal; this will make it very slippery, because sweat will not be absorbed, and dangerous accidents may be caused.

The board or tin (or "tell-tale" as it is sometimes known) is set at the bottom of the front wall, and usually has a red boarding strip running along the top.

The ceiling should have a clearance well above the specification in the rules and a minimum of 5.64 metres is suggested for good squash. Also, the lights should not hang down so far that they will impede high shots but should be set high in the ceiling to illuminate the court brightly and evenly.

If the court is a cold one, some form of heating in the gallery is recommended as squash can otherwise be an extremely cold game to watch. A cold court can adversely affect the bounce and responsiveness of the ball, making timing more difficult, and rallies less long and even less frequent.

One important aspect of any squash court or set of courts is ventilation. Without proper ventilation, walls will sweat and condensation will form.

These are just a few points about the court which may serve as a guide. However, the business of constructing a squash court is highly technical and, if you are ever considering it, you must seek advice from experts. Short cuts in construction are usually a false economy since mistakes can be very expensive to rectify. For further information, it would make sense to contact your national governing body for expert advice.

2 ELEMENTARY STROKES

The Grip

At this stage, we must assume that you are familiar with the basic principle of squash. There are two players on the court and you are taking turns at hitting the ball and in so doing trying to frustrate the efforts of your opponent in making a good return (without actually standing in his way). Thus, reduced to simplicity, your object is to strike the ball against the front wall and cause it to bounce twice on the floor before your opponent can reply to your shot. If you do that you win a point, and if you do it often enough you will win enough points to win the game, and eventually the match.

Your shot will be either a defensive measure against your opponent's attack, or an offensive measure to put your opponent on the defensive. It is important that you should understand this distinction now, because once you are on court playing, the difference between the two will be forgotten while you are more concerned with the problems of reaching the ball and hitting it effectively.

It is important to emphasize that learning to strike the ball correctly on both the forehand and backhand sides is essential. There are no short cuts and practice is the only way to achieve a satisfactory and fluent consistency of stroke. So the first thing to learn is how to grip the racket properly, in order to hit the ball most effectively. Squash is a game that demands a high degree of efficiency; consequently you must ensure that the first step is an entirely correct foundation on which to build your game. If you are a beginner and you do not learn to grip the racket in the right way at the outset, it will be extremely difficult for you to readjust later.

However, every squash player, being human, is different and you must allow your own natural tendencies to be moulded into your own style of play, so that you do not limit your horizons. This individuality applies to the grip as much as to the rest of your game. We will show you the conventional grip here but players with unorthodox ones have been known to be equally successful.

With the first purposeful wrapping of the fingers round the racket handle comes your initiation into the wonderful game of squash. Take the racket in your left hand (if you are right-handed) and hold it vertically by the shaft with the racket face facing sideways. Extend your right hand to "shake hands" with the racket handle, and settle your thumb and forefinger round it with the "V" on top. The palm of the hand is slightly behind the handle and the other fingers are spread round it to give support and solidity. The thumb should extend round the handle, ending up between the forefinger and the second finger.

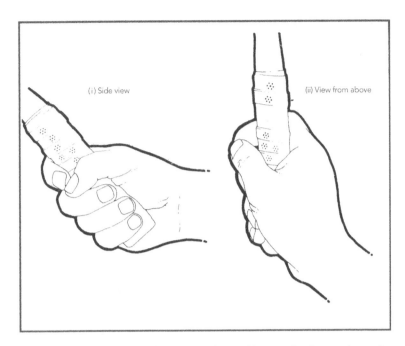

Diagram 2   The grip. Note that (i) the thumb is placed between forefinger and second finger, while (ii) the V between thumb and forefinger is almost central on the handle.

The "V" formed by the thumb and forefinger should be almost central on the centre line of the shaft of the racket but slightly to the right. The racket should be held as near to the base of the handle as is comfortable.

Once you have settled your hand round the handle in this way, swing the racket round for a few minutes to get the feel of it. Do not hold it too tightly—it is not necessary. Your grip should be relaxed and should only be tightened for hitting the ball. If you hold the racket tightly the whole time, the strain will begin to make itself felt and your arm will tire more quickly.

The Forehand Drive

Apart from the serve there are four basic strokes in squash; the drive, the lob, the drop, and the angle. All other shots are variations of these (except the volley) and all of them can be played either on the forehand or the backhand. On these strokes depends the entire structure of the game and your endeavour must be to hit with maximum effect and minimum effort. Now that you have adopted a grip that gives you the greatest allowance for the free execution of these strokes, the path ahead should be easier.

Diagram 3   The forehand: (i) backswing (ii) impact (iii) follow through.
Note that the weight is transferred from right foot to left.

The first and most important shot to learn is the drive, the basic weapon in the armoury of the beginner. Remembering from James's experience that it is not enough to hit the ball hard, you must learn to hit it with consistency and control, qualities more important than sheer strength. This is also a good moment to mention what may seem obvious—keep your eye on the ball. Many mistakes are made by average players who do not watch the ball right on to the racket.

The drive can be divided into three parts; backswing and preparation, impact, and follow-through. With your left foot forward and your feet at right angles to the side wall, you are standing parallel to the course of your shot. Adjusting your balance, your weight should start on the right foot as you raise the racket on the backswing to a point just above and behind your head. The elbow should remain bent and the wrist should remain cocked so that the racket head is held up vertically.

Your knees should be bent at this stage as you will be able to move the weight of your body more easily from right foot to left foot. The more weight you put into a shot the more powerful it will be. Swing the racket down from the backswing position above

21

and behind your right shoulder and simultaneously shift the weight of your body to the front foot, keeping the knee bent for balance. Strike the ball at a point just opposite your front foot and parallel to the front wall, keeping your shoulders square to the side wall. Be careful not to let your shoulders turn until the ball has been struck and your follow-through has begun. If your shoulders open towards the front wall before impact the ball will tend to fly off across the court instead of up and down the side wall. This usually stems from a desire to hit the ball too hard and should be avoided until you have worked your forehand drive into a well-grooved stroke.

There is a 'sympathy zone' which you need to become aware of when hitting the ball. It begins just before contact with the ball, continues during contact, and for a short distance afterwards. During this critical phase the racket path travels in a parallel plane, perhaps sometimes with a pressing motion, and is coupled with an extra effort to feel the ball on to the racket. It is critical for good timing. This may sound advanced but it should be of use to beginners as it will help you develop a sense of sympathy between the racket and the ball.

The racket should follow through continuing its arc to a point above the left shoulder, with the elbow slightly bent so that the racket stays close to the body.

The action of hitting the ball is similar to throwing one. Although the wrist should remain cocked during the backswing, it may be lowered for the moment of impact depending on the height at which the ball will be struck.

You should learn the forehand and backhand drives with the racket-face square to the front wall; do not attempt at this stage to use spin, or to cut the ball, as mistakes can easily be made. It is more important to become proficient at the basic strokes before learning sophisticated variations.

The Backhand Drive

To many beginners, the backhand stoke may seem more difficult than the forehand, but this should not be so—after all, it is easier to throw a hat at a hat-rack with a backhand swing rather than a forehand. Beginners who spend more time practising the supposedly more difficult backhand often end up with a more fluent and correct stroke than on the forehand, where the initial swing at the ball may tend to prevail because it has met with reasonable success. The backhand is an instinctive stroke.

The basic ingredients of the backhand drive are similar to those of the forehand, except that the ball falls on the player's opposite side. For instance, if the player is right-handed and the ball falls on his right as he faces the front wall, he will play a forehand; if it falls on the left, he will play a backhand. As squash is played within walls it is not often possible to run round a backhand and hit it on the

Diagram 4   The backhand: (i) backswing (ii) impact (iii) follow through.
Note that the weight is transferred from left foot to right.

forehand as can be done in tennis or, to a lesser degree, badminton. It is also tactically stupid to try this at squash as it boxes you in and greatly reduces your stroke options.

Once again it is necessary to emphasize that the proper execution of the stroke should be learnt. The wrist and forearm should follow a sweeping arc down from a high but compact backswing, with the arc from left to right. There should be no inward turning of the wrist.

As the racket sweeps down to the ball, the moment of impact corresponds to the moment at which you let go of the hat towards the hat-rack, and is similar to slapping with the back of the hand. However, the fact that the backhand is more instinctive than the forehand does not mean that you will necessarily end up with a stronger backhand stroke. Each individual player will use his own method, adapting the textbook stroke. This is merely to show you the ease with which you will be able to pick up the technique for the backhand.

Thus the stroke itself will start from above the left shoulder with the weight on the back (left) foot. The wrist remains cocked and the racket head up, with the right shoulder at right angles to the front wall. Maintain a well-balanced stance while you transfer your weight to the front foot as the racket begins its sweep down to the ball, smacking the ball level with the front foot as the full weight of the body reaches that foot. The knees remain bent and the racket follows through with elbow slightly bent, to keep the racket close to the body.

The Crosscourt Drive

As we have said, the basic forehand and backhand drives just described are the first and most important in a player's armoury of strokes. The straight drive should be played up and down the court parallel with the side wall until you have a well-grooved stroke and swing. When you have practised this on both flanks and feel you have mastered in part the essentials of timing and technique, then we can look at the next stage of the drive — across the court.

The crosscourt drive from the forehand side should be made in a similar way to the forehand drive down the wall. With the front foot forward and the knees bent you should swing the racket back, bending the elbow, and 'throw' the racket at the ball, hitting through it. The moment of impact should be in front of the left foot so that you hit the ball early by comparison with the drive down the wall. It is better to keep the racket face open for the crosscourt stroke unless you wish to 'kill' the ball, in which case you will take it at the height of its bounce, stroking down and across. If you do not want to hit the ball in the early position, the same shot can be made by leaving the ball later in its flight and pulling it back across court with a late flick of the wrist — not easy to do with complete consistency but it can be deceptive and rewarding.

The backhand crosscourt drive should be played in the same way as the forehand but from the left side of the court hitting towards the right. Crosscourt strokes can be used to deceive the opponent — and the art of making your opponent think the ball is going to be hit in a different direction plays a big part of squash. By shaping up for a forehand or a backhand drive, you can hit down the wall or across court merely by changing the moment of impact very slightly. If you hit the ball opposite the front foot it will travel parallel to the body, if you hit it just in front of the front foot it will travel across the court.

Simple Practice

This is your first introduction to tactics and at this stage it will be useful to look at some fundamental points. Nobody can learn the straight drive and the crosscourt drive merely by reading a book. It is not even enough to go and play a match in which you make some effort at following the basic principles. Winning is the object of any match, and it is an important part of the psychology of winning that you do not experiment with technique once the match has begun — so the only answer for real improvement is plenty of practice.

One of the advantages of squash is that it can easily be practised on your own and the best way to make sure that you understand

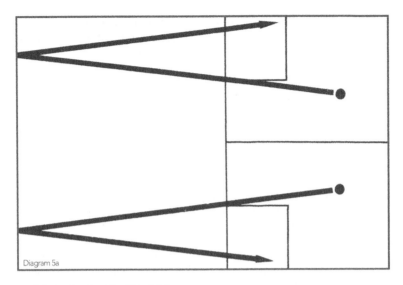

Diagram 5a

Straight forehand and backhand drives.

Crosscourt forehand and backhand drives.

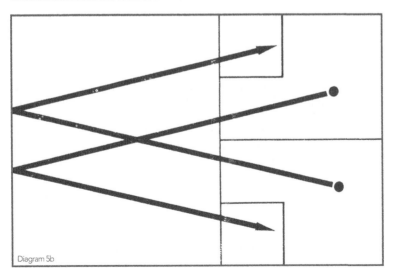

Diagram 5b

what you have read is to go into a court and practise the strokes in the same order in which you have read about them. But don't practise for too long or you may become bored.

Initial practice sessions should be taken easily and it is advisable not to try and do too many things at once. Play the ball up and down the side wall so that it bounces in or about the service box. Practise the shot until you feel you have coordinated all the necessary technique, and then practise a little more until you begin to hit every ball into the service box.

A good drive is the result of a ball hit at the correct pace and height. To take this one stage further, the most important drive is the one that is hit down the wall to bounce well before the back wall, with the second bounce dying on the back wall. The use of the wall is important, as we shall see in the next section, to prevent your opponent from being able to cut the ball off before it passes him to land at the back of the court.

The length of the drive is an important element in the effectiveness of the shot. If the length is good your opponent will only have one chance to hit it and that is before it passes him. It should not bounce off the back wall to give him a second chance. If the shot is close enough to the wall then your opponent may also be unable to stop the ball before it passes him.

In practising, the whole height of the front wall should be used to gauge the power and direction of your shots. The higher you hit the ball at the front wall, the softer it should be, but you can hit harder as you aim lower towards the tin. If you practise with this in mind then you will soon learn that you do not have to hit the ball too hard all the time. It is vital to learn the relationship between power and height when hitting the ball on the front wall, to achieve control and accuracy specifically with reference to the length of shots to the back of the court.

Concentrate all the time while you are practising, for bad practice is worse than none at all.

Practise the crosscourt shots in the same way—aim to hit the ball into the service box area to begin with, and then extend this by aiming to land the ball deep into the far corner from where your opponent will have difficulty in retrieving it.

This elementary tactic of trying to keep the ball away from your opponent will be discussed more fully together with other simple tactics later in this chapter under the heading *Basic Tactics*. Before we get to that stage we must first have a look at the service and the return of the service.

The Service
As every point must begin with a service, it is essential to practise it. It is the only shot which is played in every rally, and it must be included in this chapter before you begin to play a game of any kind.

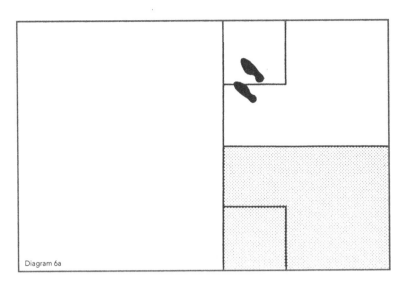

Diagram 6a

The forehand service from the right court: only one foot need be inside the box. The shaded area shows where the ball must bounce.

The forehand service from the left court: the left foot is nearest to the front wall. The shaded area shows where the ball must bounce.

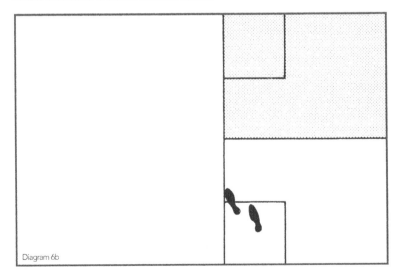

Diagram 6b

There are players at all levels who do not pay enough attention to the art of the service. Being the only shot in the game that is not a return of your opponent's shot, you are not in any sense under pressure. You should not consider it as just a method of putting the ball in play and starting a point. It is a good opportunity to put your opponent under pressure and attack the back corner even though it is extremely hard to gain a point outright with a service winner.

Having seen that the service can and should be used as an offensive shot, you must use the advantage it will give you. As we will see in the section on tactics, the art of squash is to be able to place the ball where your opponent will find it hardest to retrieve and return. We must now look at how we can put this theory into practice as far as the service is concerned.

For the beginner it will be wise to concentrate on the forehand service from both service boxes. Nearly all players prefer the forehand service although the backhand serve can be used to good effect if only to vary the way in which your opponent has to receive it. There is certainly a case for the backhand serve in the forehand court—this will enable you to keep your eye on your opponent and his movements. However, we will concentrate on the forehand serve for the moment.

There are two principal types of service in squash—the lob and the hard service. The most common and most effective of these (if correctly hit) is the lob, which we will look at first.

Don't forget that you have plenty of time—use it to position yourself correctly. The left foot should be in front of the right, whichever side you serve from, and should be nearer to the front wall. You can stand with either one or both feet in the service box but you will save yourself some movement after you have served if you stand with only one foot firmly in the box. Diagrams 6a and 6b show the ideal position of feet for the forehand serve. Place your feet solidly and stand well balanced.

The ball can be hit at any point of the wide arc which extends from your feet to above your head when your racket arm is extended. However, it is better to strike the ball from a position somewhere between knee and shoulder level and preferable at about hip level. The ball should be hit from behind and below in an upward arc which will carry it firmly towards the front wall. The moment of impact should be above the front foot.

You should aim to hit the front wall a little more than halfway across the court and about midway between the service line and the front wall line. In your mind you should mark off the area on the front wall at which to aim—an area about four feet high and six feet wide is recommended (as in Diagram 7).

The ball should continue to rise, as high as the ceiling permits, on its journey towards the opposite court and should glance off the side wall on its downward path at a point equidistant from the back

28

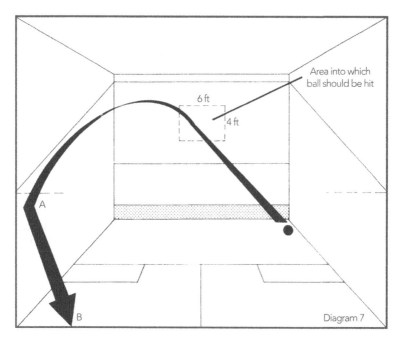

The lob service: the ball, hit from the service box, should rebound from the front wall on to the side wall (at A, approx. 4-5ft from the back wall), and then bounce (at B) before striking the back wall.

wall and the floor—preferably between four and six feet. Height is important, as the higher the ball goes in the arc after hitting the front wall, the more vertically it will drop in the far corner. The aim of the lob serve is to keep the ball so close to and high on the side wall that your opponent will find it difficult to volley before it drops.

The ball should drop after hitting the side wall and bounce before hitting the back wall. The only way for your opponent to return this type of serve is by digging it out defensively which keeps you on the offensive and well placed.

Thus the lob service is a carefully hit lob aimed to drop as deep as possible in the far corner without your opponent being able to make a good return. If the ball hits the side wall and then back wall before bouncing it will be forced out into the centre of the court, where your opponent can return it with interest, so try not to over-hit the service, or to hit the serve too low so that your opponent can reach it to volley before or after it hits the side wall. You must also avoid hitting the side wall too early as that will bring the ball out into the court as well.

As soon as you have served you should move to the T, the junction of the half-court line and the short line. This is the commanding position in a squash court and you should attempt to reach there before your opponent. (See section on simple tactics.) Remember one thing about the lob service — no power or speed is required, just technique, which can only come from considerable practice.

If your opponent seems to be able to read your serves, then you should vary them. This could be the time for you to try a backhand serve to alter the angle at which the ball comes off the front wall. The occasional variation in service may catch your opponent off guard, and surprise can often produce dividends. If your opponent is caught out of position he may have to do a block return or move in the opposite direction to that which he intended.

One of the best ways to catch your opponent in this way is to throw in the occasional hard service, the other principal type of service. This should be hit from a similar position to the lob service. The ball should be hit flat and aimed hard just above the service line; it should stay close to the side wall, hitting it close to the floor. The length of the shot should be good, i.e. the second bounce should die on the back wall.

Another variation would be to hit a hard service straight at your opponent to catch him wrong footed or to aim with a full serve straight for the back wall nick.

The principles of serving outlined here apply equally to a serve from either side of the court.

Before moving on to the return of service, let us look briefly at the requirements for a service as far as the rules of squash are concerned. When serving, at least one foot must be completely inside the service box (not touching the red line) and the ball must be hit between the service line and the front wall line. Hitting the lines in squash is "out" and therefore the ball must hit between those two lines. If you do not have one foot completely in the service box it will be counted as a fault. If the ball hits the wall on or below the service line but above the tin it is a fault.

The ball must also land in the opposite back quarter of the court (the shaded area in Diagrams 6a and 6b). If it does not land in that quarter it is also a fault. Your opponent may volley the serve before it lands in his quarter.

Return of Service
After a service, the receiver must return the ball on to the front wall above the tin. Like all other shots, the ball must not touch his body or clothing and must not be hit twice. Unlike the service, the return may hit a side or back wall on its journey to the front wall, where it must land below the front wall line and above the tin. If it does touch a side wall it must do so below the side wall line.

The object of explaining to you how to return the service is simple. It may not be as easy as a straightforward drive and it is

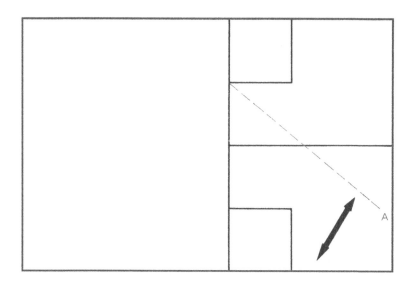

Diagram 8
Receiving service; in left court *above* and, in right court *below*. Stand at A, facing the side wall but looking over your shoulder (along dotted line) to determine the type and direction of service. Once the ball has been struck, move forward under the flight path (along the dotted line) to cut it off on the volley if possible and attack one of the four corners of the court to move your opponent off the T.

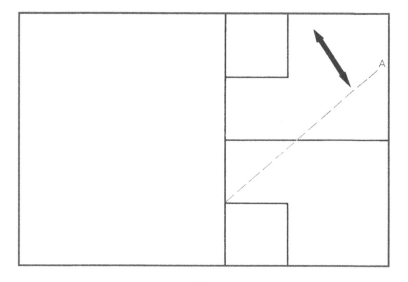

important that you learn how best to reply to your opponent's service. After all, if your opponent has learned how to serve the lob service and rarely makes a mistake, you must quickly learn how to retaliate.

As the receiver, you are under pressure from the server, whose prime objective is to make things as difficult as possible for you. He is under no pressure and has the initiative, which you have to try and gain from him by placing the ball as far away from him as possible. After serving he will have moved to the one position which dominates the court—the T. From that point the furthest place on the court is one of the corners.

The first thing to learn is where to stand so that you have the best chance to return service adequately. In Diagram 8, you will see that you should stand in the back corner near the centre line. From there you can look sideways towards the server and determine the type of service with which he will be presenting to you. As soon as he has struck the ball, you can anticipate where it is going and if possible cut it off on the volley before it lands along the back wall or in the corner. Move from your receiver's position in a line towards the nearest corner of the service box.

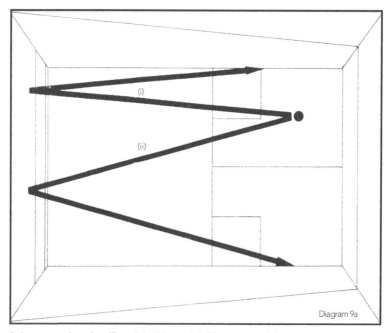

Diagram 9a

Safe returns of service: (i) straight drive or lob (ii) crosscourt lob.

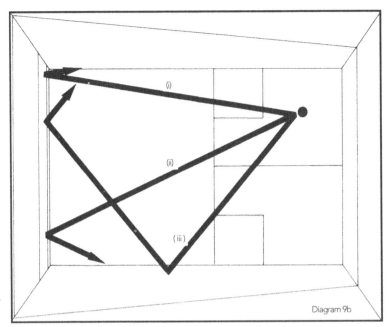

Offensive returns of service: (i) straight drop shot (ii) crosscourt drop shot (iii) reverse angle.

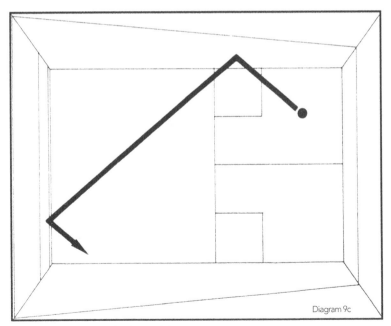

Defensive return of service: boasted shot.

The ball has to land in the receiving quarter, and working on the principle that it is easier to move forwards rather than backwards, you should not stand anywhere other than position A to receive. From there you can quickly move forward to any part of the receiver's quarter.

The safest return of service is a straight drive parallel to the side wall in your quarter, hit to a good length. This can be either a drive after the ball has bounced or, preferably, a volley. Equally successful is a lob, driven or volleyed, along the side wall to a similar length. Both these shots land in the back corner and force your opponent to move from the T towards the back of the court, leaving the T position vacant for you.

Variation is obviously desirable in returning service. However, it is vital that you master the safe returns before attempting more advanced and sophisticated shots. The other safe return is a crosscourt lob into the far corner. To be successful this shot must have plenty of height and should be kept as wide of the T (and therefore as near to the side wall) and as deep as possible. In both cases this is to avoid your opponent. These are the two principal safe returns and remember, "when in doubt, play safe".

If you decide that your opponent's serve is not formidable, as soon as you have determined the ball's direction there are three basic offensive strokes you can employ to give you the initiative. The straight drop shot to the front corner nearest to you and the crosscourt drop shot to the far front corner are both difficult shots to play with accuracy, but may provide you with the means to move your opponent up the court while you gain the T position. Both shots need much practice. They can be played either on the volley or after the ball has bounced.

The second attacking stroke is the kill which has the same effect as the drop shot in terms of placement but is hit with maximum power and can be turned into a deep drive if necessary.

The third attacking stroke from this position is the reverse angle boast. You hit the ball first on to the far side wall from where it will rebound on to the front wall above the tin and drop back on your side of the court quite far up in the front corner. The service off which you hit this shot will need to have bounced away from your side wall to enable you to get the racket behind the ball.

If a service is very good, then almost certainly the only means of return will be defensive and the use of the boast will be necessary. The boast is a shot that touches a side wall before reaching the front wall. A good service may prevent you from getting the racket sufficiently behind the ball to hit it straight down the side wall. In this case you will have to aim it at the side wall at such an angle that it will rebound on to the front wall above the tin (preferably close to the far front corner). By using this shot you can turn a

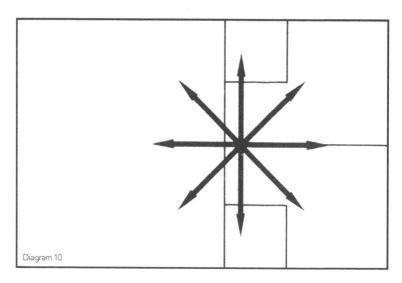

Diagram 10

Command of the T position: from here you have fast access to all four corners of the court.

difficult situation into an advantageous one by once again forcing your opponent into one of the corners. See Diagram 9c.

The boast return should be hit in the same way as a drive but the racket face should be sufficiently open to carry the ball across the court to a point above the tin; the point of impact should be between the body and the side wall.

As your proficiency at squash increases you can move forward to receive service, provided that you still cover all the possible areas. Standing a yard further in may help you to return services more easily on the volley but it may also force you to step sideways or backwards occasionally to dig out a good service.

If a service glances off the side wall on to the back wall before bouncing and the ball comes out into the centre of the court, always try to back up and return it without turning round and hitting the ball on your other side. This can be dangerous as your opponent will almost certainly be within your line of fire. If you back up towards your opponent without turning round, you have the added advantage of pushing him off the T as he has to move out of your way.

Remember—if a service is difficult to return, play a safe or defensive shot. If it appears to be easy, play an attacking shot, but keep the ball away from the T and the centre of the court.

Now for a look at the basic tactics of squash.

Basic Tactics
With the forehand and backhand straight drives as the bread and butter shots of squash, your first attempts at practising hitting the

35

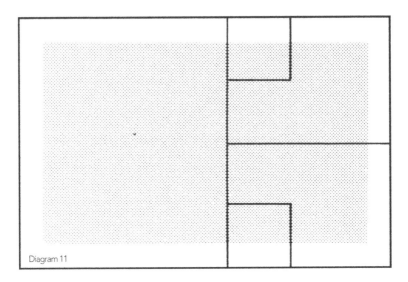

Diagram 11

Ideally, keep the ball out of the shaded area, i.e. the centre of the court.

strokes should be concerned with correct timing. Once you have mastered the timing, everything else will follow, including power. Timing is all important.

This book has so far been written as if every squash player was right-handed. Of course this is not the case but as most players are, I have catered for the majority. I apologise to those left-handers who have read so far and, before going further, would venture to suggest that you have already found it easy by now to interpret the instructions to suit your own game.

In order for you to be able to play a game we have already covered the service and the return of service and in the course of looking at these basic shots (including the forehand and backhand) we have also encountered the need for tactical discipline on court as well as technical ability. The lob, the drop shot, and the boast (angle) have all been mentioned as well, and a more detailed look at these strokes will follow.

One must first assume that the strokes already covered are within your repertoire as a player and that you can put the ball roughly where you want it with those strokes. When you are completely proficient in stroke production and technique the game of squash becomes entirely a game of tactical manoeuvre.

There are two basic principles which must become instinctive on the squash court. The first is to dominate the T position and the second is to keep the ball as far away as possible from your opponent.

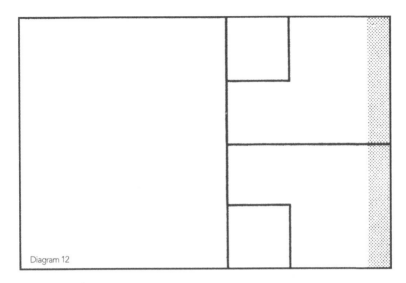

Diagram 12

A good length straight drive should have its second bounce in the shaded area.

If you can learn to dominate the T position you will always have your opponent under pressure. The T (the point where the half-court line meets the short line) is the one position from which you can move fastest to any of the four corners. As soon as you have hit the ball, you should immediately move back to the T to prepare for the next shot from your opponent. Don't stand and enjoy your own stroke, however perfect, as you will lose valuable moments.

You should never let the ball out of your sight; watching your opponent, or better still, his racket, will give you a valuable clue as to the probable direction of his next shot. As soon as the ball is hit, you will be able to react faster if you have already anticipated its direction from watching how your opponent hit it. Be on your toes, and move with the ball after he has played his stroke.

As it is your earnest intention to command the T position, it may also be in your opponent's mind to do the same. If he manages to get there first, it follows that the second most important lesson in tactics is to keep the ball away from your opponent and away from the centre of the court and the T in particular. If you let your opponent get to the T and you don't keep the ball out of his reach, he will send you to all corners of the court making you use up valuable energy. You must not let him gain a position in which he can control the rallies.

Diagram 10 shows how easily your opponent, if he is on the T, can control the entire centre area of the court. One step takes him to within striking distance of the side walls and the areas in which

37

Diagram 13

The correct stance at the T—knees bent and racket ready.

a weak return may land. In order to keep the ball away from him when he is on the T, you must hit shots that do not land in the centre of the court. They must land within about a foot of the front, back, and wide walls, forcing him to move out of position.

Always hit to a good length if you can. It does not matter how hard the shot is, provided that it lands in the right place—within a short distance of the back wall, preferably in one of the corners. A perfect length for a drive occurs when the ball does not bounce a second time; instead it hits the back wall and drops forward on the floor so that no racket can scoop it up.

When stepping on to the court for a game or match you always start by knocking up and getting the ball warm. You should hit the ball as you would in a game—don't relax just because there are no points to be won. If you usually hit the ball hard, then hit the ball hard. Find the rhythm of your game immediately so that when the match starts you know how to adapt it. Don't waste the knock-up; use it to get into the right frame of mind and to loosen the muscles. Your efforts will immediately give you an advantage and enable you to play the game your way.

Don't allow your opponent all the shots he likes in the knock-up. Just as you are trying to establish your authority, he will want to do

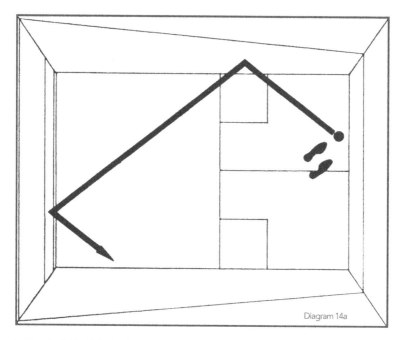

Diagram 14a

Taking the ball off the back wall: if there is not much room to manoeuvre, boast the ball off the side wall on to the front wall.

the same. So if he likes hard drives and volleys, don't give him any. Let him do his share of the work to keep the knock-up going. Don't actually keep the ball away from him—merely send him the sort of shots you think he would find hard to play so that you have the advantage when the game starts.

Tactics should always be varied from day to day so that nobody can feel that they have a psychological advantage over you because they can anticipate your tactics.

Tactics should never be the same, not only to keep your opponent guessing but also to take account of the speed of the court, the ball, the opposition, and of course, how you feel. Adapt your tactics to suit the conditions.

We have already seen the tactical purpose of the lob service—to hit the ball too close to the side wall for your opponent to volley and too deep in the corner for him to dig it out effectively (if at all). We have also seen the tactical returns of service that can be employed to make your opponent move from the T. Shots to the back corners will draw him away, and shots to the front will help him expend energy provided they are close enough to the side walls and do not bounce out into the centre of the court.

39

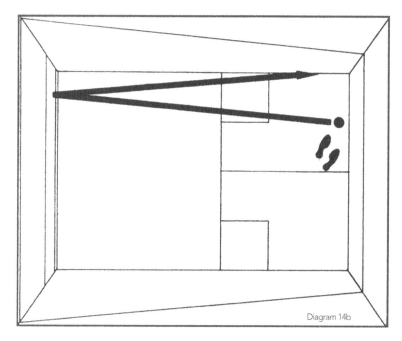

Taking the ball off the back wall: try to hit the ball straight to the near back corner off the front wall.

In discussing tactics and the T position, this is also perhaps the moment to mention the correct stance while at the T. Standing straight up with your racket trailing will not help you if you have to make a fast move. Therefore bend your knees, keep your wrist cocked with your racket head up, and remember that it is easier to move faster when you are on your toes, slightly stooping to give yourself extra "leap" potential.

The need to command the T position is now firmly in your mind and you are aware that correct positioning on the court will result in your having to cover surprisingly short distances (compared to an opponent who never succeeds in reaching the T).

When taking the ball off the back wall, you should either face the back wall or the side wall. Give yourself room to hit the ball—don't stand too close to the spot where you expect it to bounce. It may come off the back wall direct from the front wall, or indirectly via a side wall. Only a ball that is a perfect length need beat you.

If the ball lands close to the back wall and does not allow much room to manoeuvre you will have to hit it sideways and upwards, boasting it off the side on to the front wall. However, if you are restricted to the back of the court like this, try and hit the ball straight to the near back corner off the front wall (see diagram 14b).

In moving to the T position, be careful not to get in the way of your opponent if he is attempting to return the ball from behind you. If he hits you with a ball which would otherwise have gone straight to the front wall the point is his—and you are probably very sore. A squash ball travelling at speed can hurt like hell! If the ball would have hit the side wall before the front wall then the point is replayed—but it still hurts.

One last point in this chapter. If an opportunity arises and your opponent gives you a shot off which you can hit a winner, go for it but try not to muff it. In order to achieve that position you have probably worked the ball and your opponent up and down the side walls until an opening was created (possibly by throwing in a short ball to keep him guessing). If the opening looks good to you, go for the winner. If he manages to scramble it back, you still have him under pressure and nothing is lost. But don't miss it or put it in the tin—not after all the effort you have put into that one point. Error free squash is winning squash.

Summary

Before moving on to the remaining important strokes, it is worth pausing for a moment to sum up this chapter.

You have learned how to grip the racket and play forehand and backhand drives up and down the side walls and across court. You have learned how to serve and return serve. You have learned some basic tactics and the value of simple practice. Here is a short list of points to remember—if you always bear them in mind, you may have an advantage over the next man.

1 Always watch the ball—even on to your opponent's racket. (Don't stare at the front wall waiting for his shot).

2 For perfect stroke production, remember the importance of correct positioning of the feet.

3 Prepare early for your shots. Hold the racket cocked at all times so that the backswing is both easier and quicker.

4 Don't stand and admire your elegant drive, but prepare for the next one.

5 Get to the T and keep control of it.

6 Keep the ball away from the centre of the court and your opponent.

7 Vary the play. Always keep your opponent guessing.

8 Adopt the correct stance at the T, bending the knees and holding the racket ready. You are then ready to pounce on your opponent's stray shots.

Become proficient in these basic principles and you will have a foundation on which to build and develop a sound game.

3 FURTHER STROKES

The Lob

We have looked at the basic strokes and must now look at slightly more advanced, but nonetheless essential, strokes in any squash player's armoury.

When you enter a squash court and hit the ball for the first time, it is natural to hit it from below, bringing the racket from behind in an upward path. This, in its most elementary form, is the basis of the lob, which can be used as an attacking shot to win points or as a defensive shot to get out of a difficult position or to give yourself breathing space. The versatility of this shot makes it important.

The ideal lob will land in almost exactly the same place as the lob service — i.e. it will come off the side wall on its falling trajectory and will bounce before hitting the back wall close to the corner. The difference between the two shots is that the lob service must be hit from the service box, whereas the lob can and should be used from anywhere in the court. Thus, the ideal lob is one which is hit crosscourt to make use of the side wall to slow its pace before dying away right at the back of the court.

To play this shot the ball should be struck from below up towards the front wall, so that it rebounds further upwards and travels in an arc to fall as vertically as possible. Unless you are positioned close to the front wall, the ball should hit the front wall about or above the cut line but at least four feet below the boundary line. If you hit above that area you will find the ball will either go out (hitting the ceiling or roof) or have insufficient power behind it to carry it to the back of the court.

However, power and pace are not elements of the lob. The most important factor is accuracy, as you only need to hit the ball firmly enough and at the right angle for it to rebound off the front wall to the back of the court. Change of pace does have a high tactical value and exploits the height of the court.

The basic stroke for the lob is therefore the same as for a drive on either side, but the backswing should be substantial and the ball should be struck at a point in front of the front foot. The racket head may be allowed to drop below the wrist for this shot if necessary. The footwork is the same as for other shots, with the front foot forward, but the racket face should be open to lift the ball on its upward path to the front wall, and the ball should be hit from below. Hit the ball firmly — a miss-hit lob will either be volleyed fiercely if it is short, or it will come out into the court where it can be dealt with more easily if it is too deep. If you choose to hit the ball late, you will need plenty of wrist action to scoop it up.

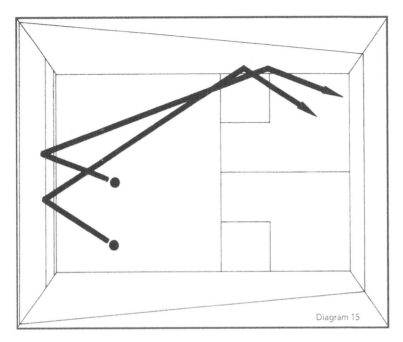

Lob from front of court: ideally this should be crosscourt. A straight lob must be of a good length and avoid the side wall above the out of court line.

In spite of being unspectacular, the lob is a most effective way of breaking up an opponent's rhythm and can give you great satisfaction—particularly if your opponent is so beaten by it that he can only stand and watch without any attempt at a return.

The object of the lob is to hoist the ball over your opponent so that, with luck, a weak return will be produced. Meanwhile you can take over the T position he has had to leave. The crosscourt lob is most effective as it makes use of the side wall to slow it down. The straight lob, while staying close to the side wall, must also be of a good length but can be more easily volleyed as the margin for error is even smaller than the crosscourt shot. The boundary line on the side wall must be avoided which usually means the ball must fly nearer the T position.

Be careful before you start lobbing that you have mentally taken in the height of the ceiling or the lights. It is no use hitting an otherwise perfect lob if you find that on that particular court the lights hang down and your lob hits one. Courts tend to vary in height.

As the lob can be used so effectively for both attack and defence, you should practice it from all parts of the court. It can be hit from either side after the bounce or even on the volley. It is also

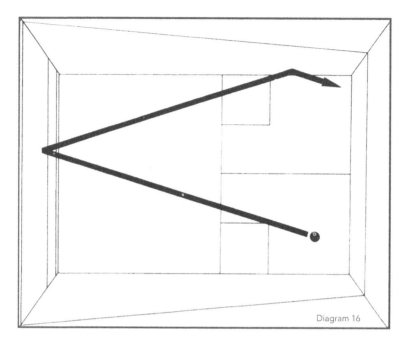

Diagram 16

Lob from back of court: crosscourt backhand.

possible and often necessary to play a boasted lob—i.e., a lob that hits first the side wall and then the front wall before rising over your opponent to the back of the court. Remember a good lob is always a safe shot. Whether played offensively or defensively, it can always become an attacking shot by virtue of moving your opponent from the T into the back corners.

The Volley
The volley is the stroke that cuts off the ball in the air before it has a chance to bounce. When you consider how much the ball is in the air and how frequently it is possible to hit it before it touches the ground, you will realise how important the shot can be.

The volley is basically an attacking shot—with it you are able to dominate the game by not allowing your opponent sufficient time to recover. The volley is also a means of returning the ball which can be an alternative to the drive or any other shot from the back of the court. Rather than let the ball travel to the back of the court and possibly create problems, because you then have fewer means of return at your disposal, you cut it off by taking it early. This does not allow your opponent any chance to dominate the front of the court.

44

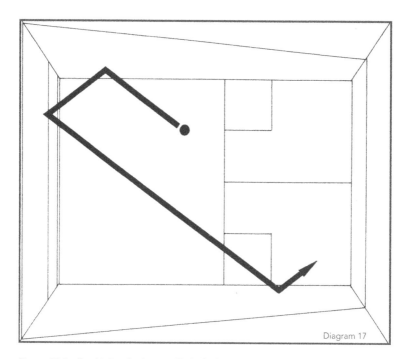

Boasted lob: after hitting the front wall, the ball rises over your opponent and lands at the back of the court.

Keep the racket head up, as the time available for backswing may be limited. The volley is a short punch with a reduced back-swing and a short follow-through. The basic shot is similar to the ordinary forehand and backhand strokes with the point of impact level with the front foot for the straight volley, though this can be varied according to the direction you wish the ball to take. The volley action, on either forehand or backhand, is a movement of the wrist and arm—you do not need to put your whole body into it. It is more of a quick reflex action than any other stroke in the game.

The volley can be used in any part of the court to great advantage, e.g. the return of service, but it is most effective as an attacking shot when you are positioned in the forecourt. Striking the volley from this position will produce many winners for you if you aim just above the tin and, preferably, close to the side wall so that the ball dies away in the nick.

The volley needs a lot of practice. Many players find the forehand volley easy but make mistakes with the backhand volley above shoulder level. It is entirely a question of practice, timing, and correct positioning as well as strength in the forearm and wrist.

45

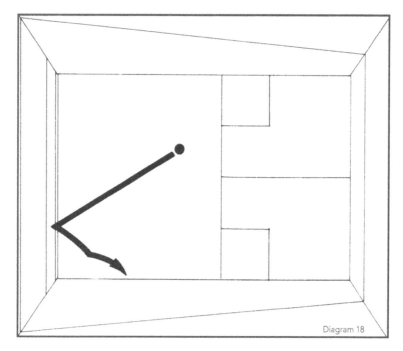

Diagram 18

The use of the cut volley will reduce the distance between bounces so that the ball will 'die' more quickly.

The volley is a key shot in top squash—the more you can volley the more you can dictate the pace of the game and save yourself a great deal of running, as well as putting your opponent under constant pressure. To hit volleys correctly from in front of the short line you should go forward as you hit the ball, having the backswing already in position (with the wrist cocked) and keeping your eye on the ball. Maintain your balance on the front foot (if necessary use your other hand to balance the body). Aim to strike the ball in midair at a point that is neither too ambitious to reach nor too low for you to be able to place your racket behind the ball. The shot can be hit with a slightly open racket face to reduce pace, or straight with a closed face to kill the ball.

The use of cut on the volley will tend to slow the ball down and can be usefully employed as it will bring the ball down from the front wall at a more severe angle and will shorten the distance between the first and second bounce. However, before learning how to cut the ball on the volley or any other stroke, learn the basic shots and be proficient in their use. The cut is executed by using an open racket face and by bringing it down and across the ball to

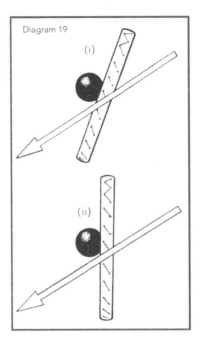

(i) Use of cut on the volley (ii) use of slice on the volley.

impart underspin. (See diagram 19.) Slice may also be used on the volley—with the same motion, but holding the racket face vertical and parallel with the front wall. The effect is similar. If you find yourself on the wrong foot faced with a volley, play safe; either hit it high across the court or up and down the side wall using an open racket face for control.

If you are at the back of the court, all the same principles apply except that you should treat the volley as a drive struck before rather than after bouncing on the floor.

The Smash
The smash is also a version of the volley and is used to prevent an opponent's lobs landing deep in the court. In order to smash correctly and safely it is necessary to maintain an open stance so that you have flexibility of direction—in other words, when you reach up and can still aim for either front corner. The weight should be on the front foot and you should bend your back to give the shot extra whip, as you may have only a short backswing. Hit the ball well in front of you, down and towards one of the front corners, and follow through fully but carefully avoiding your opponent.

The Drop Shot
The drop shot can be played on either flank like all the other principal strokes, but produces more winners and more mistakes than any other. The drop shot is a winner if executed correctly; if not, the ball will either be set up for your opponent or in the tin.

The drop shot can be played from anywhere on the court but is usually played from the front of the court, i.e. in front of the short line. Greater accuracy is possible the nearer you are to the front wall, but the principal reason is to avoid your opponent. You should usually only consider a drop shot if your opponent is behind you, for if he is in front, it would be senseless to give him a ball which is nearer him than you. However, it is often possible to play an effective drop shot from the back of the court down the side wall using the element of surprise. Don't attempt to hit a crosscourt drop shot from behind your opponent until you have convinced yourself in practise that you can not only do it but that it will be a winner.

The action for the drop shot should begin with a full backswing to deceive your opponent into expecting a drive, a lob, or any other shot for which the backswing is the same i.e. except for volley or

Diagram 20

Forehand drop shot. At this stage you are still in a position to deceive your opponent, i.e. you could play a drop shot, or a drive to either side of the court.

48

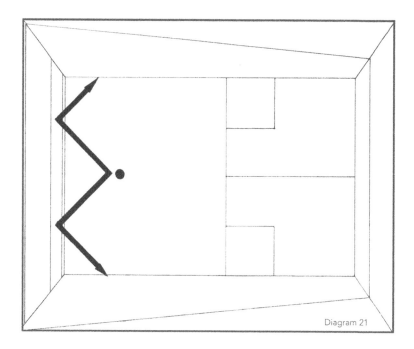

The perfect drop shot from the front of the court—into the nick.

serve. You must bend your knees and get down to the ball which should be struck at the height of its bounce—with the racket parallel to the floor and the wrist cocked. You must strike the ball firmly but softly (or else it will come out too far into the court) from behind and slightly below. The racket face should be open and the ball should hit the front wall only an inch or two above the tin before rebounding towards the side wall. The perfect drop shot is the ball that rebounds from the front wall into the nick (the join between the side wall and floor).

The positioning of the feet for this shot should be the same as for the drive—the front foot forward etc.—and the ball should be struck just in front of the front foot on to which the weight of the body should have been transferred at the moment of impact. The body should be well balanced to enable you to strike firmly but softly through the ball with a short follow-through.

The shoulder should point towards the corner into which you are aiming the ball. If the ball does not go into the nick, it is better that it hits the side wall before bouncing on the floor. This will slow it down and keep it further away from your opponent.

The best time to go for a drop shot winner is when you are at the T and your opponent is behind you, having made a return that

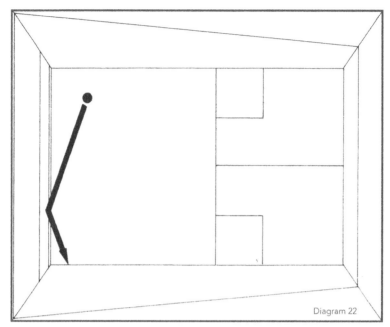

Diagram 22

Forehand crosscourt drop shot.

Drop shot from back of court: can be volleyed as a service return.

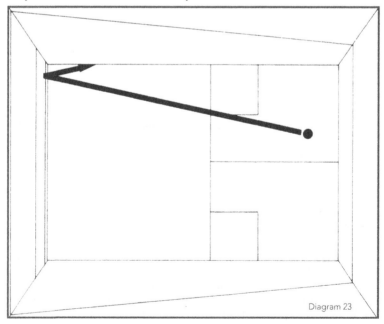

Diagram 23

has come out into the centre of the court. Your drop shot should be towards the corner furthest away from him so that he has to travel the longest distance and expend energy in doing so. In addition it moves him right up the court, leaving it open for you.

The drop shot is sometimes used after you have run fast to reach the ball, tempting you to hit it hard. However, anticipate this and move with calculated strides towards the ball so that your balance is perfect at the point of impact. This will help you maintain control of the ball.

Thus, the drop shot can be played straight to the nearest side wall (diagram 21) or crosscourt (diagram 22). You hope that both will land in the nick. The drop can also be played as a stop-volley (e.g. on return of service) which is a block shot, holding the racket out and giving the ball a short downward jab so that it loses pace. The drop can be sliced or top-spun depending on the circumstances and on your confidence.

Tactically the drop shot is a useful weapon to employ to keep your opponent guessing and vary the rhythm of play.

The Nick

The expression "the nick" is used when the ball comes off the front wall at an angle towards the side wall and lands in the join between

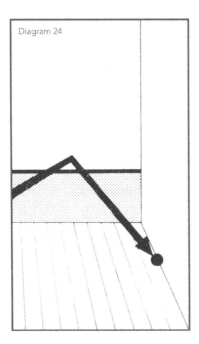

The nick: when the ball lands at the join of floor and side wall, failing to bounce — it 'dies.'

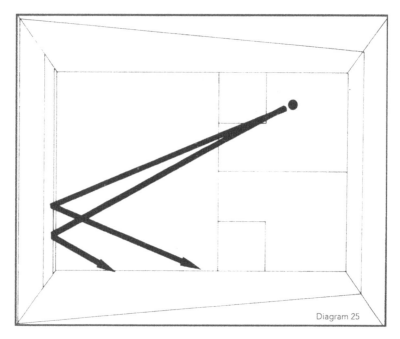

Diagram 25

The nick shot from the back of the court.

the side wall and the floor. If it is a perfect nick the ball will fail completely to bounce and the shot will be an outright winner.

The nick shot can be played from a ground stroke (after the ball has bounced) or on the volley, from the front of the court or the back. Whatever happens, an attempt at hitting the nick if you are in a position to do so is worthwhile; if it fails as a nick shot, the ball will rebound off the side wall but stay close to it and lose pace from contact. The nick is the best possible way to end a rally. A well-executed and successful nick is a most satisfactory shot and will boost your morale while reducing your opponent's.

Control and timing and choice of occasion must be perfect. As you play, you should be well balanced and well prepared with your racket at the ready position. From the front of the court, be sure you can play the shot you want—you will probably need a weak return from your opponent so that you are sufficiently well-positioned to go for the nick.

If you decide to go for the nick from the front of the court, do so when your opponent is behind you and deep in the court as if your timing is slightly wrong this will be a difficult shot for him to reach. Start the backswing early, and keep it short. Keeping your eye on the ball, your weight should come forward on to the front leg and you should strike the ball with an open racket face in front of the front leg and follow through briefly. The knees should be bent. The action in this part of the court is similar to the technique for the drop shot—of which the nick is the most important type.

The nick can also be played with great effect from the back of the court although here there is a far smaller margin for error. The ball should be struck as for a drive, but not hit fully with normal driving pace. The crosscourt drive that lands in the nick is one of the finest shots in the game, but it is also one of the hardest to execute correctly. Hours of practice must be put in before you can ever play it with regularity—let alone under pressure from an opponent in a match.

4 ANGLES

During the course of previous chapters the subject of angled shots (or boasts, as they are known) has cropped up several times in explaining the fundamental points of stroke technique and the use of the various strokes. A boast or angle is a shot that is hit indirectly to the front wall; in other words, it is a return that strikes one or more of the other three walls first before hitting the front wall.

Angles deserve a chapter to themselves; they cannot be considered elementary, and a full understanding of angled shots and practical expertise in their use can make an ordinary player into a mature tactician.

The use of the angled shot is one way to take advantage of the squash court's four walls. Whereas the basic drives up and down the court are the strokes on which your game is founded, the angled shot is more sophisticated and can bring infinitely more variety into play. The squash court is a specific size (21 feet wide and 32 feet deep) and you should learn to use every inch of it to move your opponent around and place the ball in positions which are as awkward as possible.

Apart from using the angled shot for this purpose, it can also extricate you from difficult situations. Very often, a shot hit to the back of the court is impossible to drive because you cannot move your racket round it to put enough power into the shot. The answer is to boast the ball off the side wall on to the front wall. This is a defensive measure and can be done in two ways.

For a drop shot or nick, you aim for the ball to come off the side wall and travel across the court to hit the front wall in the far front corner; or you can skid-boast the ball, hitting upwards and forwards against the side wall, with the ball then hitting the front wall above the cut line fairly close to the centre and flying on upwards to glance off the other side wall and down into the back of the court. After the ball has hit the first side wall, it should travel a path similar to that of a lob service or crosscourt lob.

It is an ideal shot to play when you are stuck at the back of the court with your opponent on the T, being forced to play defensively. The value of the angle shot is that it can be played offensively or defensively, depending on where you are in the court, and can also be used to turn a defensive position into an attacking one.

In striking the ball, the technique is the same as for a drive with the weight on the front foot at the moment of impact, a good backswing, and ample follow-through. The ball needs pace as it has to contend with the deceleration which impact with the side wall will cause. There is only one way to learn how to get the angles right and what amounts of lift you will need to carry the ball—and that is to go on the court and experiment until you are satisfied. Then practise and experiment what you have learned by trial and error until you can play the shot with regularity when you need it.

The angle shot can be played on either the forehand, the backhand, or even as a smash. It can be played from the front or back of the court. It is particularly useful when your opponent is behind you as, if you shape up to it correctly, he can easily be deceived about the ball's direction. He may anticipate a drive down the wall, a drop shot, or even a lob. He may also anticipate an angle shot but if you hear him coming you can change it. For instance, if you are in the front of the court and he anticipates (in spite of your deceptive stance and backswing) that an angle shot is to be played against his forehand side wall, bringing the ball over across the court to the backhand side wall, and he moves in that direction, you can instantly change your plan and hit the ball early down the side wall leaving him stranded. See diagram 28a.

To hit a forehand angle shot is not technically different from the other shots, i.e. backswing, good balance, wrist cocked and racket up, weight on to the front foot and knees bent, racket face slightly open, eye on the ball maintaining the wrist cocked, and follow through after hitting the ball. The moment of impact will depend on the direction you wish the ball to follow and the extent of holding the racket face open will depend on how high you need or intend to hit the ball on to the side and front walls. If you hit the ball too early you will naturally end up with a cross-court shot, and if you hit it too late your ball may not reach the front wall. See diagram 29.

These angle shots are all straight angles—i.e. a straight angle shot is hit towards your nearside side wall. The reverse angle shot is hit towards the far side wall. See diagram 27a. The reverse angle is useful as a deceptive shot—you can make the motions of playing a crosscourt drive, then instead of hitting the ball opposite the front foot you can hit it early so it hits the far side wall first and moves along the front of the court, hitting the wall and landing back in your side. Your opponent, if he has misread your shot and been duly deceived, will be left groping just behind and to the back of the T, to which position he had moved in anticipation of your drive.

These are some of the uses of the angled shot. Basically, use the angle as an offensive shot from the front of the court and a defensive shot from the back. Use the extra time these shots give you to regain position and balance.

We cannot proceed without a quick mention of the back wall boast. This is not a shot to be encouraged unless you are in severe difficulty, because it so easily sets up an opening for your opponent. If the ball has passed you completely in the back of the court and will not be rebounding from the back wall as it is such a good length, you can turn to chase it and hit it upwards against the back wall with sufficient pace to carry it over to the front wall. The pace

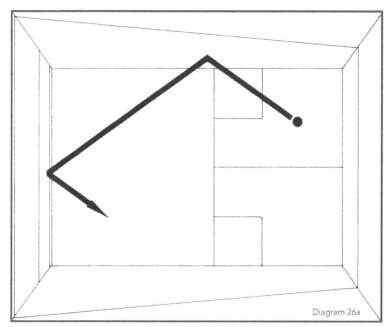

Diagram 26a

Simple forehand boast.

Boasted crosscourt drop shot.

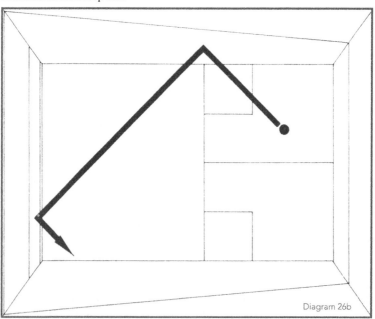

Diagram 26b

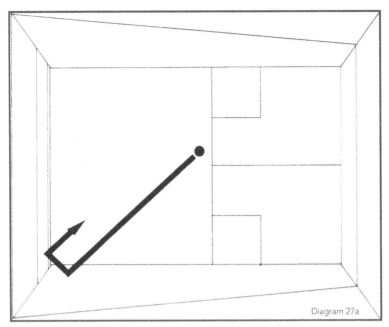

Diagram 27a

Reverse angle shot: hit towards far side wall.

Skid boast

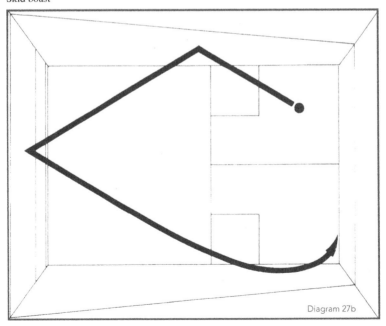

Diagram 27b

57

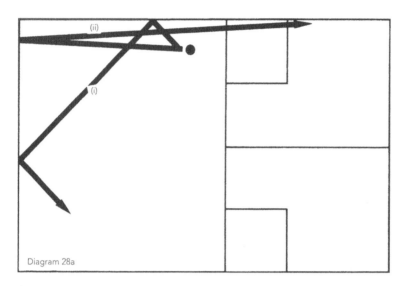

Diagram 28a

(i) Use of angle instead of (ii) drive from front of court.

(i) Use of angle instead of (ii) drive from back of court.

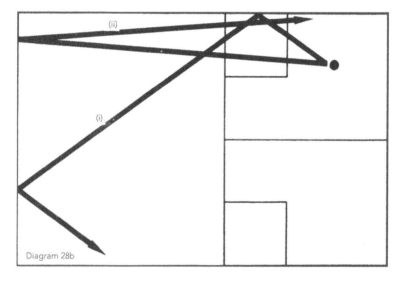

Diagram 28b

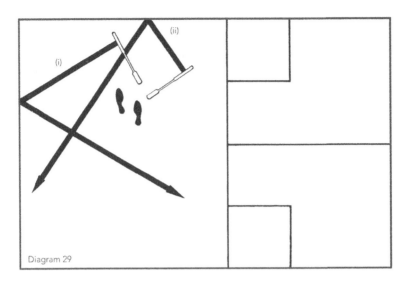

Diagram 29

Intended boast—errors: (i) the ball has been hit too early, hence a crosscourt shot (ii) too late, hence the ball hardly reaches the front wall.

Back wall boast: to be used only as a last resort, as it is difficult not to set up an opening for your opponent.

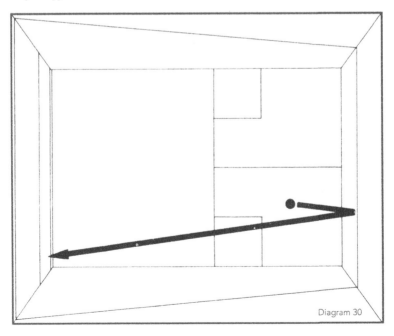

Diagram 30

at which you strike the ball is not as important as the angle. Hit the ball in a direction as parallel as possible to the side wall; if it hits the side wall and has not been struck with sufficient pace, it may not reach the front wall. The best place to aim for the ball to hit the front wall is certainly in one of the corners. If it lands in the middle it may offer an easy winner for your opponent. Use this shot sparingly—when it is the only course of action.

5 ADVANCED TACTICS AND PRACTICE

Advanced Tactics

There are so many different ways in which a squash player can hit the ball and so many variations of each shot that inevitably there are limitless ways of playing a point or rally. One of the most exciting and enthralling experiences is to watch a match between two high-class squash players each looking for and trying to capitalise on the other's weakness. If there is no obvious weakness, the struggle becomes almost intellectual as the ball weaves a design about the court that makes full use of the space available.

If and when you have mastered the various stroke techniques and are able to hit the ball more or less in the right direction (i.e. the direction in which you are aiming) then the game becomes a battle of wits between you and your opponent, assuming that he is of a similar standard. The wits required will be tactical wits, and the outcome of the match will probably depend on the tactical ingenuity of one of the players in seeking to find the most space into which to hit the ball and also to make the least errors. This presumes, of course, equal standard not only of stroke production, but also of fitness and stamina.

Basically, the art of tactics is placing the ball where your opponent will find it hardest to reach and making things as difficult as possible for him (strictly within the rules and a normal code of conduct). Your winning tactics should start before you go on court. This is not to encourage the use of strong-arm tactics in the changing room—"the last chap I played here was taken off to hospi-

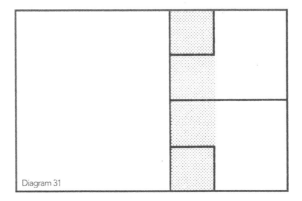

Diagram 31

Mistake area: the shaded part of the diagram shows the area where more than 50% of point-losing errors are made.

tal with blood oozing from more than one wound" type of thing. That is definitely nothing to do with squash tactics and is to be discouraged, apart from the fact that your opponent may decide to despatch you in a similar fashion.

Tactics start with your equipment. You need clean clothes, a properly strung racket, and shoes in a good state of repair. Then you must think of the background of the match, i.e. is it an individual or team event. If it is a team event, which member of the opposing team will you be playing; have you played him before; who won — and why — and how; what are his strong points. What is his forehand like, and his backhand? If you have not played him yourself, possibly one of your team-mates has. The more you can discover about your opponent before you start, the better equipped you will be in your mind about how to deal with him. That is match preparation which must form part of your overall strategy.

When you arrive at a club for a match, especially if the club is unknown to you, check the courts — the height of the ceiling or roof — to see if you can use your lofted lobs. Is it a fast court (hot) or a slow court (cold)? These conditions may have an effect on the way you want to play the match.

Tactics have been mentioned all through this book, as an early guide as to how to start moving the ball around the court, and in connection with the individual strokes. This chapter is to try to help you string together the purpose of tactics as a whole, by relating the individual tactics which can be utilised for each stroke. In a way every stroke played is like a brick in a wall; when one brick is laid, you have to lay another until you get one layer which amounts to a point. The layers are added on until you have a wall eleven layers deep—the eleven points you need to win a game. When you have built three perfect walls, then you will have won the match.

The point of looking at it this way is to see the importance of each brick in the wall, or each stroke in the rally. Do not think of each shot as it comes along—think ahead and work out how best to manoeuvre your opponent into a losing position by building up a series of strokes that will move him up and down and across the court until you can find the space into which to hit your winner. His energy reserves will be used up, which can only benefit you in the long run. If you move him around enough, he will eventually make a slip and either hit a ball that you can play for a winner, or make a forced error himself. Each shot should be a tactical part of the whole strategy you are planning to win that point.

Concentration will be required to keep the plan going and also to notice any weakness in his game. You cannot afford to let your mind wander, and you do not have time to stand and watch your shots or your opponent's. You must keep the pressure on him all the time—try not to give him time to think or plan.

Any plan must be flexible. Your opponent will certainly have different ideas about you gaining the upper hand and will do his best to keep *you* under pressure. Thus, you cannot plan more than a few strokes ahead as he will probably try to put you off your plan by introducing a devious shot or two of his own into the fray. This may put a temporary spanner in the works, but you must not allow it to deter you from subtly returning to the original plan or devising a new one. While working out your strategy, don't neglect your opponent's strong points, and the way he has played certain points or shots up until the moment in question. If he seldom missed the nick when given a high forehand shot along the side wall, then the chances are that he will not miss again and you should keep the ball away from that area.

When you start a match, use the knock-up to see if your opponent has any obvious, or even hidden, weaknesses. Also use it to accustom yourself to the court and the pace of the ball. From then on, do not stereotype your game—keep experimenting and changing so that your opponent does not become used to a particular pattern of play—although do not change a winning game plan unnecessarily. Mix your serves, giving him some lob serves, but throwing in a hard service or two for good measure. However, if he is finding your lob service easy to read and is coping with it too well for your liking, you should change it quickly and then come back to it later when it is hoped that he will be out of the habit of hitting winners off it. Change can be accomplished by altering the height, the pace, or even the direction of the service.

When the game is in progress, remember the principal points— try and dominate the T position by keeping the ball as far away from your opponent as you can in one of the four corners of the court. Go for safe shots unless a winner seems certain and keep the pressure on your opponent. Play away from him and keep him behind you as much as possible.

The art of deception should also be used in sending your opponent in the wrong direction. The backswing, footwork, and timing are vital ingredients of any stroke, and taking these items a stage further you should learn to deceive your opponent into thinking you are aiming for one shot and then playing another, e.g. shaping up for a forehand drive, then hitting the ball late and using a boast instead. Deception should be used to get an opponent moving in the wrong direction to create openings.

Gamesmanship and Tactics

Gamesmanship can be considered to be a form of tactics in most games. It appears in squash as in other games—particularly in needle matches that mean a great deal to both winner and loser. Gamesmanship is not, perhaps, the most gentle form of tactics but it can be used to good effect—if you are in need of that sort of assistance. Personally, I feel that there are two types, one of which may be used and the other which should be avoided.

The aim of gamesmanship at its most effective level is to disturb your opponent's concentration and, usually, to make him annoyed. Personally I do not like its use in this form. An opponent who tries to annoy me or upset my concentration is not the sort of opponent I will play more than once, unless forced to do so.

It is fair enough to capitalise on an opponent's condition but this cannot really be termed gamesmanship. If an opponent is out of breath, and you don't wait for him to recover, that is still fair play. By all means, keep him under pressure like that.

Equally, it is fair to play upon an opponent's weakness, such as a poor backhand volley. But you must decide whether to concentrate your efforts on hitting the ball continuously towards his backhand (in which case it may improve) hoping he will send back a weak return; or whether you should only concentrate on his weak shot when you really need to put the pressure on and gain a point.

In the same "fair" category must come the question of age. If your opponent is older than average for an active squash player, it stands to reason that although he may have years of guile and cunning that he can use to good effect on court, he is also less agile and his legs will not last as long as they used to. Move him around, make him stretch, bend, and run, for these are legitimate means of tiring your opponent and gaining the upper hand.

Gamesmanship is not cheating, although sometimes it is so close to it that the distinction is almost imperceptible. Remember one thing—very few, if any, champions have had recourse to the art of gamesmanship to help them win. They have been far too concerned with vital aspects of their own progress to stoop to methods that might be considered dubious.

Practice

Squash has an immediately obvious advantage over nearly all other games because you can practise alone for as long as you wish. All you need is a court. It may not be so enjoyable to prac- tise like this, but there is no doubt that it is the only way to really improve and perfect your strokes and your ability to vary their use to fit the occasion. The maxim "practice makes perfect" may be a bit corny but it still holds true. Practice can also provide you with plenty of exercise if you are sufficiently self-disciplined not to be lazy about it.

Most people practise too little and play too much, though oth- ers find practice as invigorating and enjoyable as playing. The main object is to improve, but the exercise value will also do you good.

When practising, be sure that the strokes you are playing are the correct ones—it is just as easy to learn faulty technique on a stroke as good technique. Groove the shots rhythmically until

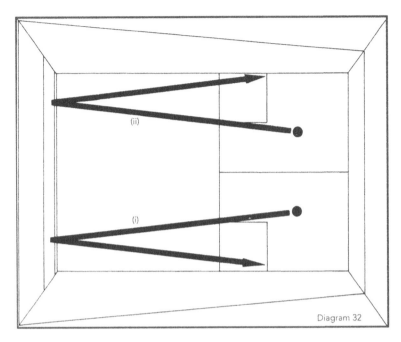

Practising (i) forehand drives and (ii) backhand drives: stand just behind the service box and hit the ball up and down the side wall.

Ball control: stand at A and hit the ball so that it bounces between the dotted line and the short line, then try drives to the back of the court, i.e. into shaded area.

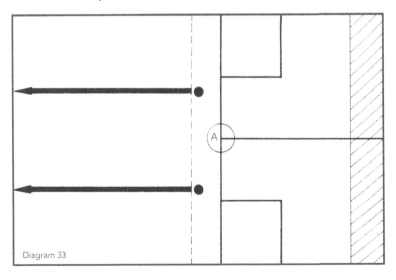

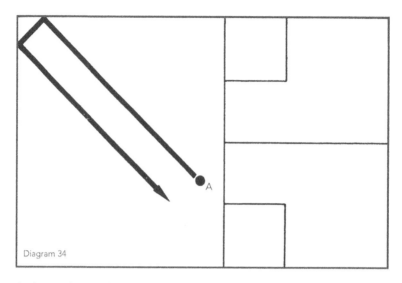

Diagram 34

Angles: stand at A and play the ball to the side wall by the forehand corner so that it returns to you. Repeat.

they become automatic. We have looked at all the strokes in the book—now it is for you to practise them—first alone, and then with a partner.

Ball control must be high on the list of priorities for practice. Until you can control the ball, you will be lost. Irrespective of where you are and how the ball is hit to you, can you hit it in the manner and direction that you have chosen? You need good reflexes to move into the correct position to hit the ball at all, apart from hitting it in the right direction. To do this well you must learn ball control by constant practice.

Learn to use all the dimensions of the court to move your opponent around; place the ball where he is not, or where he will find it hard to reach—either by a direct shot, or by a deceptive shot which will make him change direction. Ball control is needed for these manoeuvres—control before power or pace should be your maxim.

A lucky shot is something you cannot practise. Desperate lunges at the ball may result in occasional points, but do not rely on them to win matches for you. Don't bother to practise the blocked service return hit off the frame. If you do it in a match be thankful you were lucky enough to hit a return at all and practise the real thing afterwards.

Control, timing, flexibility in changing the shot after you have begun the backswing, change of pace—all these points should be practised in conjunction with the shots. Practice conditions should be similar to those for a match and your mental discipline must force you to work hard at it. Only if you have experienced real pain in terms of hard work in practice sessions can you hope to have the stamina and graft to outlast a tough opponent on court.

Each shot should be attempted from a new position with variations of pace—and of course you must work at these shots from both the forehand and the backhand sides.

Several short practice sessions are thought to be better than a few long ones. It appears that between sessions, provided that they are frequent, the theory is that the mental processes are able to absorb knowledge which increases the ability on court after the interval. In other words, after one session has finished the mind will continue to absorb knowledge from it, so that there may be a marked improvement in performance between one session and the next as long as the interval is not too long.

Individual Practice

Practice on your own is obviously harder work but in the long term it will certainly be worth it. To begin with, use the practice sessions to groove your strokes and gain experience while also introducing the possibilities already mentioned, such as change of pace and height.

The first stroke to practise is the drive. Place yourself in the forehand court just behind the service box and hit the ball up and down the side wall. Each shot should land in the service box. Practise until you get 10 out of 10 shots in the box. This will help you acquire the instinctive ability to hit the ball to a reasonable length.

Next, practise the same thing with the backhand drive. Don't worry too much about the pace until you have found the length; then increase the pace. Divide the drive into sections—before, during, and after, and go through the technique for each section carefully, applying it studiously to the practice sessions. The drive into the service box cannot be practised too often.

As an additional ball control measure, move forward to the T and practise hitting the ball so that it lands about three feet from the front wall. Imagine a line parallel to the short line a yard up the court and hit the ball back to yourself somewhere between the imaginary line and the short line. This is merely useful for ball control as you are close enough to the front wall for a short hit with pace to make you react fast to return the ball satisfactorily to the front. Your reflexes and ball control can be improved by gradually speeding up the process until you can carry out this exercise at a fast pace five or six times consecutively.

Then move your practice to the side walls at the back of the court. Stand about four feet in front of the back wall and practise your drives up and down the side wall. Try to hit to a perfect length as much as possible and try to keep the ball up and down the side

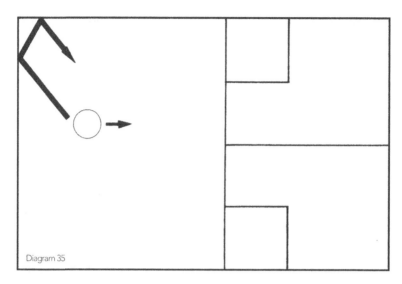

Diagram 35

Drop shot: start 4ft from the front wall and work slowly back until you reach the T.

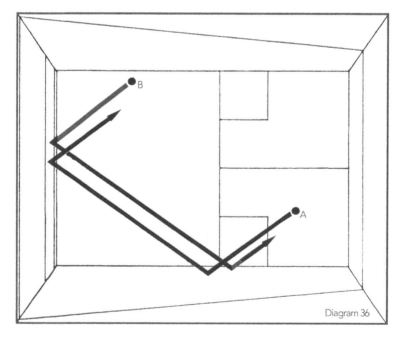

Diagram 36

Practising in twos: A hits a boast from the back of the court, while B returns with a crosscourt drive to the side wall.

68

wall. When you begin to find it really difficult to return the ball, you are making good progress—for in other words you are beginning to beat yourself.

In practising the drive you can also practise hitting the ball from the same position early, at the top of the bounce, and late—but in the same direction, i.e. not using the early position to bring the ball round as in a crosscourt forehand. This will help you develop the use of the wrist in determining the direction of the shot.

Moving on from the drive, practice sessions should always include serving. The service is the only shot in the match for which you have time to prepare. It is probably less interesting practice, being less active than the other shots, but it is still most important.

Don't go on practising until you are bored. If you do, the benefit of the session may be lost. Only continue for as long as you find it enjoyable and interesting.

Individual practice can include angle shots, volleys, and drop shots. For angle shots you should position yourself to the left and slightly in front of the T. (As in diagram 34.) Play the ball to the side wall by the forehand corner and it should come back to you so that you can continue to practise the same stroke.

With volleys, stand about six feet from the front wall and hit the ball to and fro without letting it touch the floor. Gradually increase the distance from the front wall and try to keep the ball going in the air.

The drop shot can be practised quite far up in the front of the court. Start four feet away and work slowly backwards until you are practising from the T (diagram 35). All these variations will give you the ability to repeat the shots you need in a match, after much practice.

Practice with a Partner
By practising with a partner you can repeat many of the exercises which you set yourself as an individual. However, as those exercises are probably better practised on your own, use the time you have with a friend to do something more constructive.

The most useful form of practice in twos is to have one player in the front of the court on one side and one player at the back on the other. With this formation you can practise the lob, the boast, the drop, the volley, the crosscourt drive, and so on. As you have a partner you can keep pressing him as if he was an opponent, trying to beat him through accuracy of shot and control although each of you is only allowed to use one basic stroke. This creates the right atmosphere and will assist both of you to concentrate harder (diagram 36).

To repeat—the most important thing to practise in order to improve is hitting the ball to a good length. Unless you are able to do this, you are unlikely to go very far.

6 COURT BEHAVIOUR AND SAFETY

It is important to realise at an early stage that both you and your opponent are moving around at speed in a fairly confined area. Your opponent will often be very close to you and sometimes too close for safety, whether he is in front of you where you can see him, or behind you where you cannot. You must learn to limit your swing in such a way that the racket does not become a dangerous weapon.

You and your opponent must ensure that you give each other room to play and that you do not hinder each other's right to return the ball. Be particularly careful with the follow-through which has been known to cause severe injury. It is not necessary when you are at close quarters for your racket to continue its follow-through at the same pace after the ball has been struck. This should diminish in pace and you should attempt to keep your racket closer to your body and under control. In spite of the small area in which squash is played, it is quite easy to play safely and still enjoy the game just as much. Don't allow your, or your opponent's, enjoyment of the game to deteriorate because of dangerous play.

You should always arrive a few minutes early for a match or even a friendly club game. This is not always possible, but you should always intend to leave a few minutes spare between arrival at the club and going on court to play. You may need to park the car, or your bus or train may be delayed. Too many club players tend to arrive at exactly the moment they are due on court. They have rushed to get there, have to pay the court fee before playing, and to change, and consequently arrive on court five minutes late. Not only is this bad manners to your opponent but you have also missed valuable court time. Quite apart from that, you will already be out of breath and flustered while your opponent will have his eye in and his mind on the game.

If you are playing in a match, you are allowed five minutes for a knock-up. Use the time to have a proper one, and accustom yourself to the feel of the court and the ball. Allow your opponent an equal number of balls to hit. There is nothing more annoying than having a knock-up with someone who never seems to send you any. Offer to change sides when your opponent indicates he has had enough of one side.

When the time comes to open the match, if you are serving make sure that your opponent is ready to receive. Do not begin until you have looked over and seen that he is in position.

Once the match has started, the important thing is to keep out of your opponent's way. The correct tactical approach is to head for the T position at the first opportunity by forcing your opponent away from it, ideally into one of the four corners of the court. Do be reasonable about your right to the T position. There is no reason why he should give it up if you have been unable to manoeuvre him away with a good enough shot. Likewise, if you are dominating it, don't move if you can legitimately keep your opponent at bay.

If your opponent asks for a let, give it to him — it is better not to argue. You may feel that he doesn't deserve one, but if he is able to ask then he must feel that he does. If you feel he was wrong, try not to let him have any more by keeping out of his way. Also, if you hit your opponent with either racket or ball, apologise properly and offer him a let if the occasion justifies it or if you yourself would expect a let in similar circumstances.

Another important point to consider in terms of court manners is when you are obstructing your opponent, albeit by mistake, from taking a shot at the ball. Don't wait for him to ask for a let; give it to him automatically if you know it is your fault.

If you are in front of your opponent at any time and the ball is his to return, then if he hits you it is his point if the ball would have gone straight to the front wall. Therefore it is obviously better (and more comfortable) to keep out of the way.

If there is doubt about whether a ball was up or not, it is always better to play a let unless you have a marker who can make the decision for you. Never knowingly take a point for a ball that has bounced twice or that you have hit twice.

One last point. If you wear glasses and you are taking up squash, you may like to consider the advantages of contact lenses. It is perfectly possible to play squash wearing glasses but unless you are extremely careful they may slip and be broken. Also, if you happen to be playing a rather wild opponent, there is a chance that in his enthusiasm his racket may dislodge your glasses and possibly cause injury. Not only may you feel less vulnerable wearing contact lenses, but some people claim that vision is improved more with them than with glasses.

7 FITNESS AND TRAINING

Fitness

Squash requires a good eye, a strong arm and wrist, great movement and considerable judgement for success. However, one of the most important aspects of squash today is fitness in terms of stamina, strength, speed and agility. Of all modern sports, squash has one of the highest rates of energy expenditure.

Fitness for squash consists of increasing the efficiency of the heart, the muscle cells, the circulatory systems, the lungs, and so on. As far as the heart is concerned, fitness will require an increase in the heart muscle's size; with muscle cells, the volume of muscle must increase; with the circulation, the blood will need to move faster in greater quantities to the right areas; the lungs will need increased capacity, and the body will need to be rid of excess fat. All these organic improvements can be achieved by taking regular hard exercise which will result in an all-round improvement of body efficiency, including more stable heat dispersion. Heat loss can be a problem if you are unfit, resulting in a too-fast rise in temperature, which can be dangerous. If you are fit, heat dispersion is more regulated, taking a more even course.

Fitness also means that agility, coordination, reflexes, and balance are all at their peak. The degree of physical fitness depends on general health and nutrition. One cannot be physically fit without a balanced diet of proteins, fats, carbohydrates, minerals, and vitamins. In other words, eat plenty of fruit, meat, fish, eggs, fresh vegetables, salads, cheese etc.

Moderation in both food and drink is recommended. Modern scientific dieticians recommend very limited consumption of alcohol, even beer and wine: it can be genuinely harmful to the system, however enjoyable it may be at the time. However, in my view there is nothing wrong or harmful about the occasional glass or two of wine or beer, but not before playing. In fact, if you are competing in a match it is suggested that you decline offers of alcohol for the previous 24 hours or so. Never play on a full stomach. Be sensible about what you eat within a few hours prior to playing. There are, of course, exceptions to the rule, but by and large you will find it more comfortable not to eat anything heavy two or three hours before playing.

Smoking has been proved to be positively harmful to health generally. It is also particularly bad for the sportsman who needs all the capacity his lungs can give him and therefore it is discouraged.

Fitness refers principally to stamina; the best way to increase yours is by running, which is covered in the training section of this chapter.

Speed is another element of fitness. Without it you cannot hope to return to the T fast enough, or to reach the ball if it is hit away from you. Anticipation and quick thinking can save you some energy but unless you are playing somebody who cannot take advantage of your sluggishness (in which case you are very lucky) you will need to develop speed. This is covered in the next section as far as circuit training is concerned. However, there is a test you can do with a friend to develop both your speed and general fitness. Take a box of old squash balls on court (12 balls) and empty them out all over the court. Then time yourself running round and picking them up. Then let your friend do it. Do this two or three times, each time trying to do it faster. When you start again next day or a few days later, try and beat the previous fastest time. This exercise need not, of course, be done on the court.

If you have not played squash before or if you have not taken any exercise for a long time, start gently. Hit the ball around for 15 minutes or so on the first day and gradually build up. It can be disastrous to take violent exercise all at once when you are not used to it. Your heart may not like the sudden extra work it is being made to do, or you may pull a muscle you did not know you had.

Sleep
The amount of sleep required by an individual will vary depending on occupation, age, and possibly sex, although it is not clearly established that men require more sleep than women. Some people require at least eight hours sleep a night while others are able to survive on far less. Some people, too, are able to restore themselves with short naps of a few minutes at a time. If you are used to a certain pattern of sleep then it will be hard to break it — you will find it tiring to change until a new pattern becomes a habit.

Once again, we encounter variations that depend on an individual's way of life or metabolism. If your job entails using your mind, it is generally thought that you will require more sleep than a manual worker. Young people certainly need more sleep than old; in fact, it can be said that as you grow older you require less and less sleep, although the average requirement for an adult is estimated at about eight hours per night — thus one third of your life should be spent asleep in order to get the most out of the remaining two thirds.

Occasional lack of sleep will not have any detrimental effect but regular loss will result in tiredness and lack of concentration. You may also become short-tempered. However, it is unlikely that permanent damage will arise from consistent lack of sleep and the ill-effects it causes, as nature usually intervenes well before such a stage is reached. One really good night's sleep can help you "catch up" on a considerable deficit.

Sex

A great deal has been written about the effect of sexual intercourse on the sportsman. However, I do not propose to go into detail in this book on the subject of sex and sport. There is nothing to suggest that sex will have a detrimental effect on your squash-playing provided that you have allowed sufficient time after sex for the body to readjust itself. A good night's sleep after sex will be perfectly sufficient to allow your body the readjustment period it needs as well as sufficient sleep in normal circumstances.

Naturally, there are exceptions to this rule. Apparently, at least one world record has been broken by an Olympic champion within an hour of making love. If you wish to experiment on your own individual possibilities, it is recommended that you do not do so when you have a particularly hard match on court to follow.

Travel Fatigue

A short note on jet lag may be appropriate to the transatlantic or long-distance traveller who also plays squash.

The body has its own time clock that works on a 24-hour cycle, tuned to familiar rhythms at home. When the pattern of living changes by being transported to another time zone, the body system is thrown upside down as it tries to live life to the old system while you are imposing a new system and clock. Adjustments to new environments and timings can take up to about a week.

There is no cure for this. However, it is best to try and attune the body slowly to the new system, avoiding an abrupt change. Don't try to play squash within 24 hours of arriving. It may be physically possible, but it may not be sensible.

Training and Sports Science

Physical training is an important aspect of the committed squash player. The importance of fitness must not be underestimated as a core element of playing squash.

Modern developments in the attitude towards training show an ever more scientific approach and it is recommended that consultation with a fully qualified physical training expert is the best way forward.

Most modern squash clubs offer such a facility as part of membership and, failing that, there are many state of the art health clubs.

With an ever more scientific approach to physical training and preparing for squash matches, it makes sense that if the physical training methods have benefited from the improved scientific support now available, then mental preparation through the help of a sports psychologist is also paramount to the delivery of optimum on court performance. Equally, fuelling the bodily engine with diet and nutritional advice is crucial as well. At the elite level, playing squash successfully has become a 24 hour a day job, as it is in any top level sport, and the competitive edge is delivered increasingly with heavily researched expertise and scientific data in the various areas mentioned above. For the club player, it is important to be aware of these possibilities and the potential benefits from seeking such advice, even if it is merely for living a healthier lifestyle and the enjoyment of playing confident and competent squash. But it is not essential for playing and enjoying the benefits of competitive squash. A squash coaching professional can usually give a valuable summary of the science involved in performing well at club level; it is only when ambition runs high that sports science in all its various guises becomes attractive, if not essential.

Matches are increasingly analysed tactically with the aid of computer technology to narrow down one's opponent's strengths and weaknesses, whereas historically this used to be based on the instinct of the player or the help of the long suffering coach/friend/parent in attendance. Improved performances and results have seen the ever increasing use of such technology. Biomechanics is the scientific aid to improving technique and can be delivered through video analysis in the same way as tactical insight can be gained from seeing matches played back on video.

8 MATCH PLAY AND CHAMPIONSHIP SQUASH

Once the technique of hitting strokes correctly has been mastered, squash reverts to being a game, in common with many others, of strategic wit and stamina. Provided that the physical strength is also there, with concentration you will win points. Squash is a fast game, and the need for tactical expertise will be forced upon you by any opponent of a reasonable standard. In order to bring all your tactical experience to bear upon a match, you will need to concentrate hard, not allowing your mind to wander.

Concentration and determination are complementary, and one will be wasted if the other is missing in a player. That would be a gap in any player's match-playing ability, for it is these two characteristics that help a champion on his way to the top.

When you are playing in a match, do not let your eyes or mind wander from the court. Keep your eyes focused on the ball (or your feet if the ball is not in play), and try to ignore interruptions.

There are many factors that help a squash player to become a champion. Real pleasure in actually playing squash must be a contributory factor. Few, if any, champions at any sport reach the top level without enjoying what they are doing. The effect of success makes it even more enjoyable, just as constant failure can have the opposite effect.

To reach the top, few players can afford not to be perfect in terms of technical and tactical expertise. Beginners have everything to learn and advancement will only come if the tuition is good. The basic strokes must be grasped before additional more sophisticated techniques are learnt. Tactics then begin to play a role, and gradually a player's thinking must concentrate more on tactics than on stroke production. Stroke production should be nearly automatic. A champion develops when all these points are second nature to him and this can only come from years of hard slog and practice.

Practice probably consumes most of the time required for improvement. Consistent improvement comes if every practice shot is executed with controlled physical effort and applied thought. You must be completely dedicated and involved.

Attention to detail also plays a vital part. A champion will not only check that all his equipment is perfect—that the tension of his racket stringing is correct and that his racket handle has a fresh comfortable grip—but will also pay attention to minute detail of strokes and tactics. Attention to detail in the quality and quantity of diet also plays a part for champions.

The will to win and determination and drive that go with it make up an important part of the psychological armoury of the complete player. The "killer instinct" as it is known is important in key matches when the outcome of one point may change the course of a match. Nerves at the moment of truth can ruin an otherwise brilliant player's career.

So now you are ready to play a match. Obviously there are many points to remember which have been mentioned during the course of the book and which we will not repeat now. But do remember to run after every ball—if you don't, how can you hope to win the point? However you scramble it back, your opponent may miss it—always remember there is a chance.

Playing matches is a natural sequel to learning the game. Any sport, apart from the exercise value, is supposed to instil competitiveness in you, which is what match play does.

Squash reflects the true personality of a player, because everything happens so fast that he has to revert to his natural self. If you are casual, it will show in your playing, and similarly if you are determined or aggressive.

Matches are the proving ground of all your endeavours on the squash court, and this chapter is to help you fulfil your ambitions to win matches. If you know that you are playing a match at a certain time on a certain day, take care not to have a large meal on that day until after the match. Have a light lunch and consume enough fuel to keep your engines running at full pitch for the match. Ensure that whatever food you eat on the day is full of protein and nourishment. If you have had a steak the evening before, then that will be beneficial to your dietary fitness for the match. Also ensure that you get your full quota of sleep the night before a match—too little sleep, however fit you are, may begin to tell towards the end of a long match.

The subject of clothing has been covered in the early part of the book. If you feel brighter and happier when you are dressed in smart and trendy clothes, why not bring that feeling on to the court as well? Wear clean shirts and shorts, for apart from feeling sharper you will be a credit to your club if you dress smartly.

Attention to detail as far as your racket is concerned has also been mentioned. It may be that you are the proud owner of more than one racket, in which case take it with you and ensure it is in as equally good condition as the other. It would be unfortunate if your racket broke and you had to resort to another which was uncomfortable to hold and had poor tension in the frame. It might cost you several points before you become used to the change.

Do not forget your pre-match tactics. Study your future opponent if you have a chance before playing. Do not watch the ball but watch him—and closely. When his pattern of play emerges you can then plot and plan your tactics against him. If you have not had a chance to watch him, when you go on court you must watch the knock-up and the early stages of the match to find out how he plays. Keep an open mind on your opponent at all times. Don't plot too studiously as equally he may have watched you and devised a special pattern of play for the match—it may be quite different from the pattern you have seen. Clues to look for are whether he tightens up or becomes nervous on certain points; whether he is a good volleyer; if he can cut off the ball in mid-court; if he presses home his advantages when in a winning position; whether he falters overhead, how tough he is when losing—whether he fights back desperately; what his weaknesses are, and so on. These are some of the questions to which you must know the answers. Once armed with this knowledge you can plan a bit further ahead.

In preparing yourself for the match, you must impress upon yourself the importance of *efficiency* on court. The only way to be as efficient as you possibly can is to reduce your margin of error to a minimum. Play a simple basic game—do not aim *one* nick above the tin if you do not *always* hit it above the tin. Aim one foot above for safety to reduce the margin of error. Play all the shots at your disposal safely and try to keep them in the four corners of the court. Efficient play is a stable foundation on which to base your game.

Always try to win by playing your own game and imposing it on your opponent, irrespective of your style of play, be it aggressive, dependent on accuracy, or consistency. The chances of winning a match when you have adapted to the style of your opponent may be limited. Always play within your capabilities and do not foolishly try to do more than you are able.

Play against your opponent's game, not his name or reputation. A determined effort against one who enjoys a better reputation than you is more likely to unsettle him. He has everything to lose and you have a reputation to gain. This is one of the principal reasons established players lose to those who are less well-known; a good effort shakes them and allows an element of doubt to creep into their minds, causing uncertainty in their play.

Successful match-play depends upon finding your strengths and knowing your weaknesses and making the best of your knowledge. If you find you are losing, try not to indulge in a little self-recrimination and decide the reasons. If your tactics are wrong, try to change them. If it is simply because your opponent's shots make it impossible for you to carry out the right tactics, then try to appreciate the fact that you will have to improve—there is always room for improvement.

Perhaps a little more pace on your shots, giving your opponent less time, will unbalance him and disturb his rhythm. You can achieve this either by hitting the ball earlier or by hitting it harder. Experience will show you what to do although the basic principle remains the same.

If you are winning, then keep on with the same tactics and perseverance. It is surprising how many apparently "won" matches are lost by imprudent changing of winning tactics.

Assuming that you have practised your shots, that they are working well, and that you are fit, then concentration may be the one single factor that separates a good player from a bad one. Concentration varies among individuals and you must work to improve yours if it is something you find difficult. Never let your concentration slip in any circumstances. It can pull you out of the most depressing situations.

Remember that your opponent is human too and that he has feelings and reactions the same as yours. If you are in a tight position, don't forget that he may be suffering in the same way. Tension and physical exhaustion can affect him just as much as you. Don't isolate yourself from your opponent—keep fighting in case he is the first to crack.

You are there to win—so don't go out there to be a good loser.

9 MARKING AND REFEREEING

Interest in squash over the years has resulted in more individuals playing the game and players and clubs becoming more interested in competitions, tournaments and leagues.

All serious competitive squash matches should be controlled by a marker and a referee. A marker quite often handles the game almost completely, and in fact if there is a shortage of officials at a particular event, he may double as a referee. The marker calls the score and makes the decisions while the referee, if there is one present, may be needed to adjudicate an appeal from one of the players on a decision made by the marker. Interpretation of the rules is also a referee's job, and the principal reason for his attendance.

The referee may interrupt a match if he thinks that the marker has made a mistake, or if he feels that a player has infringed the rule on fair view of the ball and freedom of stroke. If the referee thinks a player has not made sufficient effort to get out of the way of his opponent, then he can award a point to that opponent. If a player does not allow his opponent to have a fair view of the ball, i.e. if the ball is shielded by a player after it has hit the front wall in such a way as to prevent his opponent from seeing it quickly enough to make a stroke at it; or if he crowds his opponent by standing too close without actually obstructing; or if he prevents the opponent from having the whole front area of the court to aim for, then the referee should allow a let. However, if the referee thinks the player has done one of these three things deliberately rather than negligently, then he should award a penalty point to his opponent.

There is one more instance in which the referee can make a ruling. If a player is prevented by his opponent from making a winning shot, then the referee should award him a point. It will depend on the referee's experience how he estimates whether a winner could be produced from certain situations; for this reason, it is more or less essential that anyone who marks or referees a squash match also plays or has played and/or coached the game to a reasonable standard so that he understands the sort of situations with which he could be faced in making a decision.

These points are covered fully in the rules of the game at the end of this book. Obviously, if you are marking and/or refereeing a match, you must first have a clear working knowledge of the rules. Marking and refereeing are both important jobs in squash and not without interest. If you are an enthusiast, neither is a difficult task. A working knowledge of the rules is easy to acquire, because if you play, you will already know a good many of them. National governing bodies organise courses which are worth attending if only to learn a bit more about the game.

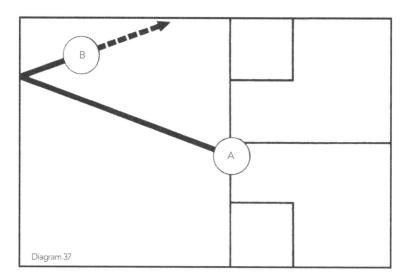

Diagram 37

If the ball hits B before he can return A's shot, then B loses the point.

If B (intentionally or not) prevents A's shot from hitting the front wall directly. A wins the stroke.

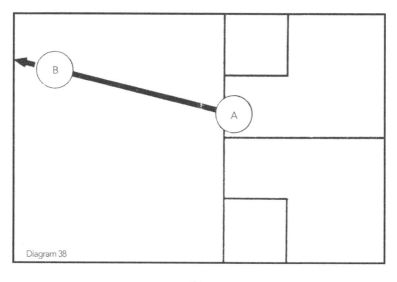

Diagram 38

81

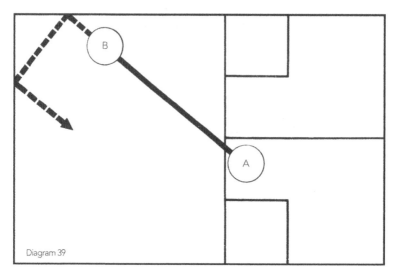

Diagram 39

If B (intentionally or not) prevents A's shot from hitting the front wall indirectly, then a let is played.

If A's shot hits B, but the ball would not have reached the front wall anyway, then A loses the stroke.

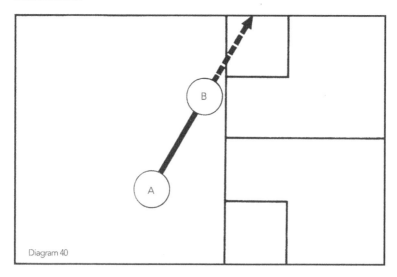

Diagram 40

It will take some time to acquire sufficient knowledge and confidence to mark top-class squash, but small beginnings often lead to other things—and there is a need for markers and referees to assist at competitive events at all levels. Confidence is needed because you will be required to make quick decisions, instinctively showing that you know what is right or wrong. If you have no confidence in your judgement, your players will certainly have none.

There are many refinements that a marker or referee will need to learn, but it must suffice to simplify the let and penalty situation. If a player is intentionally obstructed he is awarded a point; if it is accidental but he could have hit a winner, he is awarded a point; if it is accidental but the ball could have been returned then a let should be played.

Most of the points a prospective marker or referee needs to know are in the rules. It is not the intention of this book to go into greater detail on the subject. However, a marker should obviously apply common sense to the rules and when he has learnt all the correct calls he can begin to apply his knowledge.

One thing must be remembered. Very rarely have I heard a marker from the back of the gallery state the score sufficiently loudly for all the spectators as well as the players to hear. Quite often only the odd half dozen people close to the marker, apart from the players, can hear it. Everyone there will want to know, so speak loudly and clearly.

There are qualifications which need to be achieved in order to mark or referee at the highest levels.

It is worth noting that three referees are now regularly used in professional squash worldwide.

10 COACHING

The popularity of squash has resulted in there being many players and insufficient officials to cope with the demand. However, coaching is a different matter, for this is not ideally a part-time or amateur occupation. A very reasonable living can be made from it and there is a good supply of qualified professional coaches.

Coaching is both worthwhile and interesting. In recent years there is a far greater emphasis placed on the importance of coaching and it is now usually considered as a valued profession. This chapter is for those who may be interested in learning briefly how to start coaching beginners. It is possible to attend courses run by the national governing body to qualify as a coach and this is a highly recommended course of action for anyone interested.

It is not necessary to have been or to be a top squash player to become a teaching professional. However, you do need to be proficient and technically correct at all the strokes and at explaining elementary tactics and the rules. In fact, top players are often unsatisfactory at coaching or teaching individuals who have only just started to play because they have forgotten what that stage was like in their own careers, and cannot bridge the gap to an understanding of the pupil's problems.

Communication with the pupil is of vital importance—the ability to get across to him what you want him to learn. Since every pupil is different, the coach must be able to communicate easily with all types of people.

When taking a beginner on the court for the first time, you should first introduce him to the various parts of the court. It is not necessary to go into great detail about all the lines at this stage but a quick mention of the front wall, the tin, the short line and the front wall and side wall lines should be sufficient to keep him playing in the right direction.

You have probably already helped him choose a suitable racket—not only suitable for a beginner, but also taking into account his economic situation. Before actually starting to hit the ball, you should of course show him the correct grip. Explain to him why that particular grip is the one to use and why it is successful.

Then place the pupil in the forehand court approximately on the short line and hit the ball to him off the front wall, suggesting that he returns it in a similar way. You may find you have a pupil who has played tennis, badminton, or cricket already, and who knows a bit about ball games and coordination of movement. So much the better. Alternatively, you may find you have somebody who initially seems quite uncoordinated, and who does not respond in the same way at all. In the latter's case, it is a question of perseverance;

you must be patient and keep sending him the ball until he finally clicks. You must obviously help as much as you can and try to correct his mistakes—he may not have his eye on the ball or he may be aiming for a ball that bounces higher than the one you are using. Whatever he is finding difficult, you are there to help him.

It is always easier to teach beginners individually so that you can focus your full attention on that one pupil. It may be that you can teach three or four beginners at once if there is a shortage of time or courts, but be careful that you teach them all safety in the court and court manners just as well as you would an individual pupil. Court behaviour is important and should be discussed at an early stage, while safety *must* be discussed at the beginning of the first lesson as soon as your pupil has swung a racket for the first time. Accustom him to the fact that the racket can be dangerous and cause injury right at the beginning of his squash career, and he will remember it.

Pupils of any age, particularly younger ones, have a limited learning capacity in a concentrated period. Generally, half-hour periods of continuous coaching are quite sufficient. In fact even better would be two periods of 15 minutes each, with a 15-minute gap in between. The increased learning capacity that this introduces is remarkable. However, that is usually impractical.

Concentrated coaching does not mean half an hour of solid talking about how to play. You should divide your time carefully into sections so that a few minutes talking is followed by a sustained period of action on the court. If all the instruction is theoretical rather than practical, the pupil will become bored and his mind will wander, defeating the purpose of the lesson. So talk for a short while, then demonstrate, then let the pupil try. Most people learn faster by seeing and doing rather than reading or listening—this applies particularly to squash.

After the elementary start, the first stroke should obviously be the forehand. It should be followed by the backhand and then the other shots in a reasonable order, e.g. service, return of service, lobs, volleys, drop shots, and angles. In teaching all of these strokes be sure to point out the basic footwork necessary, the back swing (safely), the hitting of the ball (correct moment of impact), and the follow-through.

It is important to keep the pupil feeling that he is enjoying learning the game and that he is improving all the time. Don't let him feel uncomfortable at any time—even right at the beginning you must make him feel welcome, that you are personally interested in his progress, and that he has nothing to be self-conscious about. This is all part of the job of communication; the pupil will learn best in a happy and enthusiastic atmosphere.

Part Two

11 EARLY HISTORY

The game of squash is generally thought to have had its origins between 1820 and 1840 at Harrow School in England where boys waiting to play the game of rackets hit a softer ball against some walls outside the court.

Squash is really the younger brother of the game 'rackets', which was first recorded as being played at Harrow in 1820. The dimensions of a rackets court are considerably greater than those of an international standard squash court and rackets is played with a very hard ball whereas squash uses a soft ball, with which the name of the game is associated.

The two sports are so closely related that for more than two decades in the early 20th century they came under the jurisdiction of the Tennis and Rackets Association which was formed in 1907 to administer the games of Real Tennis, Rackets and Squash. Eventually, the Squash Rackets Association (SRA) was formed in London in 1928 and the sport began to spread.

It is possible to trace the development of the game of squash back to the origins of ball games but it is beyond the scope of this book to offer anything like a complete history of an exercise so ancient and cosmopolitan. It must suffice to give the briefest of histories on the relationship of squash to other ball and racket games.

It is known that in the 13th and 14th centuries the game of tennis (real, royal or court tennis—whichever you prefer) was played in France as a means of recreation and exercise. Tennis continued to be played throughout the centuries and was truly called the game of kings—Francois 1 and Henry V111 were two of the many monarchs who used to play.

Rackets developed indirectly from tennis as a ball and racket game which could be played by one person hitting a ball against a wall. Apart from Harrow, a version of rackets used to be played by the debtors in Fleet prison in London.

Squash soon developed from the earlier versions of rackets and in about 1860 a game was first played which historians claim is the modern origin of the game of lawn tennis. There is no doubt that this new game took not only its name from the original game of tennis.

For almost half a century after it was formed the SRA ran the game not just in the United Kingdom but in the dozen or so countries to which it spread.

As late as 1934—twelve years after the British Open had begun—the Encyclopedia of Sports, Games and Pastimes was claiming that "the authorities regard a court 42 feet long feet long and 24 feet wide as excellent."

Had courts been built to those dimensions squash would not have prospered as it has. The dimensions of an international standard squash court, originally laid down by the Tennis and Rackets Association in 1922, were confirmed by the SRA as official seven years later—32 feet long and 21 feet wide. These dimensions are still the same today.

However the delay in standardisation brought repercussions. Other governing bodies had already been formed—the United States Squash Rackets Association in 1907 and the Canadian Squash Rackets Association in 1911. These administered another version of squash, with a harder ball and courts of different dimensions, but hardball squash did not last the test of time.

In 1967 an international governing body, originally named the International Squash Rackets Federation and founded by seven countries (Great Britain, Australia, Egypt, India, New Zealand, Pakistan and South Africa) was formed as the sport was growing exponentially. Today as the World Squash Federation it has nearly 200 member nations.

Dropping "Rackets" from its nomenclature indicated that the game had transcended its origins and was entering a new and dynamic phase which turned it into a global sport.

12 THE STATE OF THE GAME

Some of squash's most dramatic matches have taken place where Robert de Niro dragged Charles Grodin to justice across New York's Grand Central Terminal, and where Cary Grant was pursued past the famous clock with its convex opal faces.

However the sport's most stunning location has undoubtedly been in Egypt, before the ancient Giza pyramids, the oldest of the seven wonders of the world, from where the spirits of the Pharaohs are said to have travelled to the heavens. And some of its most significant tournaments have been quayside at Hong Kong harbour, where a panoramic sky-line towers over the deep waters which flow glitteringly towards the beckoning expanse of China.

These three great highlights represent three different avenues of progress for squash—via the entertainment world, the promotional world, and the business world.

Such progress has brought within sight the most ambitious destination of all, the Chinese market, which is the biggest and fastest-growing. Squash is increasingly well equipped to reach it.

That is partly because the professional game has made spectacular innovations, more than any other significant sport, which are positive influences on how it is played and presented.

Rallies are faster and tactics more varied, the ball is more visible on TV, and the action more impactful. Transparent courts are easily demountable, and can be presented in iconic environments where no other sport can go.

These dramatic venues draw the viewer's gaze towards more than the squash. Cities, venues, and landmarks are promoted and enhanced by images which the tournament makes possible. And these features create new commercial possibilities.

Innovation was the theme of several presentations which the World Squash Federation (WSF) made to the International Olympic Committee (IOC). It was able to claim the sport can contribute to the Games in special ways. This, along with the IOC Presidency of Thomas Bach, who has a more flexible attitude to new sports, began to open a door for squash.

The rewards, with the potential of increasing financial support and a future transformed, are considerable. So how did squash evolve into a sport which the IOC recognised?

All-glass courts, enabling as many as 4000 spectators to view the action from all four sides, are part of a technological revolution which includes ever-advancing digital TV technology. Transparent walls allow multiple camera positions which convey the tremendous speed and athleticism of the top players. The broadcasting of squash, which used to be problematic, has advanced rapidly and the sport has become compelling to watch on TV.

This has been paralleled by other significant changes which have added to the increased attraction of squash.

Shorter, simplified point-per-rally scoring made matches faster and easier to follow. A lowering of the tin by two inches in the men's professional game increased the playing area at the front of the court and made matches more creative.

Wood was replaced by synthetic materials and made rackets lighter, stronger and larger, offering increases in power and control, and encouraging risk-taking in shot selection and tactics.

The decision-making tension between players and referees was reduced and turned into a promotional advantage. Three referees were adopted instead of one, and a video review system was added. This still allowed for a little verbal drama, but added exciting visual entertainment for spectators to the likelihood of better decisions.

As these evolutions spread, the top level game saw five continents produce world champions. There were times when every continent had representatives in the top 20 of the men's and women's world rankings, which meant many more nations could get a player on to a medal podium.

That made squash attractive for any multi-national Games, and heightened the sport's profile further. Successful appearances at both the Asian and Pan-American Games were followed by a great impact on squash's debut at the 1998 Commonwealth Games in Kuala Lumpur.

The men's final between Peter Nicol of Scotland and Jonathon Power of Canada was so thrilling that squash got more worldwide television coverage than ever before. That breakthrough altered perceptions about squash as TV entertainment and further enhanced its Olympic potential.

Squash had become a sport on the move.

Courts are relatively easy and quick to erect, making squash an ideal venue-sharer with other sports. Squash is simple and economic in other ways too with only 64 athletes and 20 officials being needed for a multi-sport Games.

Steady progress has also been made by the Professional Squash Association (PSA), which runs the men's tour, and which expanded to 500 player members,120 events and almost 3 million dollars in annual prize money.

The Women's Squash Association (WSA) tour, with about 250 players, 100 tournaments and 1.5 million dollars is also following an upward curve. This made possible an increasing number of joint women's and men's tournaments, some with equal prize money.

The women's game also enjoyed phases of spectacular publicity, partly because it showcased two of the world's most talented athletes.

Heather McKay, an Australian who won 16 consecutive British Opens, was undefeated for almost two decades in the '60's and '70's, usually demolishing opponents for a handful of points. No-one in any sport has done anything like that.

Forty years later, Nicol David became the highest profile player ever. The Malaysian's record of world titles had increased to seven by 2013, as her reign as number one approached 100 months. Her exceptional fame owes something to the fact that she is the first Asian woman to reach the top, and a fascinating cultural cosmopolitan mix—a Christian from a predominantly Muslim country, with a Chinese mother and an Indian father, and based in Europe.

One male transcended the sport—Jahangir Khan, who was unbeaten for five years and seven months during the 1980's, reviving the legend of the world-beating Khans from Pakistan. Squash's shop-window has had some spectacular wares to sell.

For many years there were encouraging trends at the grass roots level too. A century and a half after the first squash court appeared in England, in 1864, about 50,000 courts have been built worldwide. The boom years started in the 1970's in the United Kingdom, spread in the '80's to Europe, and moved in the new millennium to Asia and the United States.

The sister sports of table tennis and badminton became part of the Olympic programme in 1988 and 1992, and the boost to their funding made clear that squash should intensify its efforts to follow.

It became recognised by the IOC, joined the Association of Recognised International Sports Federations (ARISF), and became part of Sport Accord, an umbrella organisation for multi-sports games.

The WSF also opened an executive office in Lausanne, where the Olympic headquarters are located, a move which helped fine-tune the sport's bid for inclusion at the 2020 Games in Tokyo.

In traditional squash-playing areas, such as Europe, Australia, and Pakistan, a steady base of enthusiastic players continued to thrive even as a number of alternative leisure and cultural activities emerged, the most pervasive of which was the social media phenomenon.

The escalation of property values in some cities meant the area occupied by a squash club could generate a bigger commercial return in other ways and a good example is the squash club I co-founded and built in central London in 1972 which was converted into a successful fitness club several years ago.

England ceased to be the only major focal point for world squash but it still has the largest participation and now a well resourced governing body too, which helped England become the first country with both men's and women's world champions—Nick Matthew and Laura Massaro—for 28 years in 2014.

Matthew has been at the forefront of British squash for several years and has had good company in the form of James Willstrop who also became world number one. More recently, Massaro has emerged as a major challenger for top honours, becoming the first English woman ever to win both the World and British Open titles.

England still has the most courts, about 8,500, and there are ten nations with a long squash tradition which have more than 1,000 — Germany, Egypt, USA, Australia, South Africa, Canada, Malaysia, France, the Netherlands, and Spain — and more than 200 nations with at least one court.

Some intriguing new squash nations have also emerged, including Poland and some other Eastern European nations, and in Asia, Hong Kong, Singapore, and Malaysia among other countries, have made significant advances. Hints of major progress have also appeared in that most lucrative development target, China.

Two of the sport's most influential nations, Egypt and the USA, have advanced by very different means and with different outcomes.

Egypt surged unexpectedly during the era of Hosni Mubarak, the Egyptian president. A squash enthusiast, he saw a way of elevating his country's international profile by utilising its great squash tradition going back to the 1930's. Government funding helped the sport become popular again in Cairo and Alexandria.

Coaches, club competitions, juniors and top level players all prospered. Egypt achieved such spectacular success that it had five of the world's top ten men. It has also developed some top level women players, a remarkable achievement in a male dominated culture.

Egypt utterly dominated the world's top junior competitions and seemed likely to win the top titles indefinitely. But the situation changed with the political upheavals of the Arab Spring in the region and support for squash suffered accordingly.

For decades the USA had been the bastion of a different form of the game — hardball squash. Faster, but with somewhat less variety, it had seemed more compatible with the substantially narrower court which was the standard there in earlier years.

But hardball squash did not develop, largely because it was not played elsewhere. However, Canada was enthusiastic about softball squash and staged two world championships, and from the eighties onwards softball squash spread throughout North America. Softball's longer rallies made a better workout with greater variety and tactical sophistication, and transparent courts created a greater opportunity for spectators to enjoy the sport on TV.

By 2014 the USA had the world's fastest increase in softball squash, with an estimated growth of over 80 percent over a four year period. Participation rose to 1.2 million and continues to increase.

Many of the best coaches moved to the US, as well as leading players who turned to coaching. Lower and middle range tournaments proliferated, and top level PSA and WSA tournaments developed. The most notable is the Tournament of Champions, superbly presented by John Nimick, certainly the world's most creative and successful squash promoter, inside the cinematically and architecturally famous Grand Central Terminal in New York.

What were the cultural influences behind this boom? Forbes, the American business magazine, suggested "squash is considered one of the fastest and most demanding sports of all," and called it "the world's number one healthiest sport."

This was because of its power and finesse, movement and skill. These are time-honoured qualities which have endured despite all the technical and technological changes. In the 19th century they attracted the elite schools of Britain; in the 21st they thrive in commercial North America.

Nevertheless adapting is more vital than ever. Like many sports, squash is faced with the constant challenge of repositioning itself in an explosively diverse global market.

It has worked hard to commend itself to millions who have many new options for their leisure time. It is capitalising on the excellent impression it has made with the IOC. It has been brilliantly inventive. And the future is looking very positive.

13 HOW THE GAME IS RUN

The increased profile of squash in the late 20th and early 21st century has resulted in its organisation becoming more extended world-wide. Squash had gained in international significance both as a sporting entertainment and as a pastime enhancing good health and its leadership needed to reflect that.

The importance of the World Squash Federation (WSF) grew steadily as more countries took up squash and then as the WSF's status within the Olympic movement made development even more crucial.

The WSF is the world governing body of the individual national associations which are in turn responsible for running squash in each individual country.

Membership of the WSF has climbed to nearly 200 nations—a substantial increase from the nine which met to found the federation in 1967. That was the year of Jonah Barrington's first British Open title, at a time when competitive success depended entirely on phenomenal individual effort.

All member nations of the WSF are recognised either by their national Olympic committee or by their ministry of sport, which has made funding more reliable, better planned, and usually dependent on clearly defined targets.

The structure of the WSF was enhanced with national associations becoming part of five regional federations within the WSF, whose management became the responsibility of the executive board, which oversees day-to-day control and is supported by an executive committee on strategy and policy. Professional staff are employed to implement decisions.

The WSF is able to draw on expertise from a variety of committees, with representatives from regional and national federations as well as the two player associations, the Professional Squash Association (PSA) and the Women's Squash Association (WSA), whose connections with the WSF grew stronger. Together the WSF, the PSA and the WSA co-ordinate the world calendar.

The WSF has created several committees which handle various aspects of international squash governance. These include committees with responsibility for all business relating to Major Championships, the Olympics, Development, Courts and Equipment, the Rules, Anti-Doping, Ethics and Disciplinary Matters and Promotion and Publicity.

The relationship between the WSF and the PSA, which represents the men players and runs the men's tour, and the WSA, which represents the women and runs the women's tour, are crucial. These three organisations are responsible for the showcase events which are the lifeblood of the sport's promotional base.

The PSA also introduced SquashTV, another significant step in promoting the sport. It provides the opportunity for anyone in the world to watch top level squash at any time, both through live and on-demand footage from the association's website.

The PSA offers guidance and support to other partners too—such as players, sponsors, tournament organisers and host cities.

The WSA evolved differently. Its tour continued using the traditional 19-inch tin, whereas the men's tour changed to a two-inch lower tin in the 1980's, and to point-per-rally instead of traditional hand-in, hand-out scoring. The women did not use point-per-rally to 11 until 2008.

As standards rose, female players combined improved athleticism with a particularly high skill factor, producing styles of play often quite different from the men's, and creating a very successful image. Coloured, patterned, and attractive clothing, as well as outgoing personalities, ensure that the women are well received everywhere they go.

Part Three

THE PLAYERS—ALL TIME GREATS

Hashim Khan

Hashim Khan is often said to be the father of the modern game. That is not just because the great Pakistani won the last of his seven British Open titles little more than a decade before the professional era emerged. It was more because his dashing, high-paced style was a foretaste of the sport's increasing physicality during the 60's and 70's.

You could hear his shoes squeaking on the floor and almost smell the rubber burning, it was said. Barrel-chested and chicken-legged though he was, Hashim was fast. So fast, he often had no need for subtlety. He would simply overwhelm even those opponents who played cleverer shots, although it was also evident that he had the skill if necessary to develop them himself. But he knew that speed—speed of foot and pace of shot—would prevail.

In this way Hashim won 45 tournaments and helped change the way top level squash was played. Although two great Egyptians, Amr Bey and Karim Mahmoud, won six and four British Opens respectively, neither influenced the game as much as the Pakistani did.

Yet amazingly Hashim is said not to have competed outside the Indian sub-continent until after he was 35—although he never knew his age precisely. This was, he said in his amusing fashion, "for reason, me not born in hospital."

That was because his tribe occupied a wild region of the Khyber pass, from whence his family moved to the plains near the North-West frontier, settling in a village called Nawakille. It was in the nearby city of Peshawar that Hashim is said to have been a ball boy for British army officers, retrieving shots which were skewed accidentally over the walls of open air courts. It was after the death of his father, the chief steward at the officers' club, that Hashim's liking for squash turned into a passion. He was only about eleven.

But his biggest break hinged on good luck, not bad. The High Commissioner selected him as a last moment substitute to represent Pakistan in the 1951 British Open. It was an uncertain and debatable decision at the time but one which helped change the course of squash history.

When the then little-known Hashim thrashed the younger but more experienced and more elegant Karim in the final, he returned home a hero. After repeating the feat the following year he helped develop his brother Azam, who won four British Opens. This might have become more, for the talented younger sibling is said to have honoured the Pathan custom of deferring to seniority. Nevertheless the momentum was created for a Khan dynasty which dominated squash for 12 years, and then resurfaced more than a decade and a half later with the onset of Jahangir Khan.

Jonah Barrington

Jonah Barrington started the ball rolling. More accurately, he started the money rolling. When squash's first full-time player took a plunge into the unknown in 1969, he was a lonely prophet of a sport with no circuit, no television, no world championship, and no obvious pathway forward.

That is the piece of history for which Barrington should perhaps be most remembered, maybe even more than for the ground-breaking capture of six British Open titles in the late sixties and early seventies. These were nevertheless achievements which generated publicity for squash like never before.

Barrington brought the birth of professionalism. He did it as much by force of character as by the force of his squash. Although he was an extraordinary player, it was as a driven pioneer, a passionate talker, and an inspiring visionary that he arguably achieved more.

Having reached the pinnacle of the sport in the late 60's and early 70's, the Anglo-Irishman embarked on a planet-circling sequence of clinics, tours, and exhibitions which laid the foundations for a world circuit across five continents.

Barrington was a star wherever he went. He was refreshingly forthright, a magnetic raconteur, a great humorist, and an incisive commentator. He loved words and ideas, he was chatty, he had radically new thoughts, and he was unafraid to be controversial.

He also committed himself to a ferociously strict regimen—initially perhaps as mental therapy for his earlier drift, but then because it enabled him to last matches better than anyone else.

Barrington would hit the ball above the cut line for long periods in order to create a pressuring length whilst minimising error. This might be punctuated by the occasional angle or a skilfully tight backhand drop, but these were usually only risked when the opponent was pinned well back or starting to tire.

To some at the time it all appeared spartan and obsessive. However what Barrington did was not merely intense but well thought out and directed. The depth of his analysis, especially of the physical effects of his tactics, and of the effects upon the psychology of his opponents, made him a harbinger of modern sports science.

In this way he helped change how the game was played—at all levels.

Geoff Hunt

Geoff Hunt was not only a great champion, nor just a great pioneer, nor merely one of the greatest legends. He was arguably the world's best player for longer than any other man.

Superbly athletic, well organised, fast, accurate and adaptable, the Australian bestrode squash for long stretches between 1969 and 1981. In the process he helped to transform it, and move it into a new global era.

It was a phase during which the best were discarding amateurism and standards were rising. Despite this Hunt captured eight British Open titles when it was the world's leading tournament, and won the first four World Open titles. He became the sport's first world champion at the age of 21 and then its oldest male world champion at the age of 33. The quiet and friendly Australian just went on and on.

Much of this was due to his ability to evolve. Hunt not only continued Hashim's legacy of physicality and speed, he added to it. He would often begin matches quietly, acquiring accuracy, before tightening his stranglehold and erupting into bursts of dismissive power. A crisp cocktail of speed, power and accuracy was one description of his early style.

Impressive as this was, Hunt became a better player in the mid to late 1970's after his duels with Jonah Barrington. The improvement was a function of the very long rallies—mesmerising or attritional depending on your viewpoint—which these two played.

Hunt eventually adopted a similarly disciplined training regimen to Barrington's. He used 400-metre interval training, theorising that this most nearly represented the duration of the hardest rallies in those days. Each track lap was followed by rests of decreasing lengths. By today's standards it may seem crude, but back then it was breaking new ground and accelerating the entry of more scientific information into squash.

During the last phase of Hunt's career, during which Jahangir Khan's high tempo squash challenged him and his ability to recover after two hour matches gradually reduced, he became more adept at the lob and change of pace, which helped him contain more economically.

Even these tributes do not convey how remarkable Hunt was. According to Squash Australia, he won 178 of the 215 tournaments he contested—stats which may well be accurate but are still as improbable as they are phenomenal. They too underline not only the frequency of his successes but his remarkable longevity.

Jahangir Khan

Jahangir Khan won a record ten British Open titles when it was still the world's best tournament, as well as six World Opens, and became the player most often lauded with the accolade of the greatest ever. Its aptness is blurred because more myths and tales have attached themselves to the astonishing Pakistani than any player before or since.

Jahangir is part of the fabled Khan dynasty which started in the fifties with the great Hashim Khan, a distant relative whose exploits heralded the onset of modern squash, and continued with his father Roshan Khan, another British Open champion of the fifties. It was then revived, paradoxically, by the death of his elder brother Torsam Khan, a top ten player who suffered a fatal heart attack on court in 1979, and included his cousin Rahmat Khan, who gave up his own career to coach Jahangir to his record-breaking achievements.

These included becoming the youngest World Amateur champion at the age of 15, the youngest World Open champion at 17, and the youngest British Open champion at 18. It was followed by a sensational unbeaten run of five years seven months and one day. This is said to be the longest winning run by any athlete in professional sport, although the number of successes, sometimes said to be 555, was never actually recorded and is probably less. A legend spread, and gained irrational credence, that he was born to achieve what he did. His name, after all, does mean emperor of the world.

The truth though involved many contingencies. It was made clear to Jahangir that, with Torsam gone, the image and prestige of a nation now depended on him. This was a frightening burden for someone so young, and bearing it possibly cost him his adolescence, but he carried it manfully and with extraordinary dedication.

Nobody trained harder than Jahangir. He did it on many surfaces, sometimes in London, where he was based, sometimes in Pakistan, and sometimes at altitude. Muscular, focussed, and disciplined, he developed a blitzkrieg style in which he played at a supercharged pace for at least an hour. By that time most opponents were blown away. If they weren't, there was a brief phase of containment characterised by relentless line and length during which Jahangir would re-group his energies, before the attacks would begin again, in disconcerting pulses this time.

Later Jahangir shared world dominance with his unrelated namesake Jansher Khan between 1987 and 1991. Two years after that he retired, becoming a very popular President of the World Squash Federation, and eventually its Emeritus President.

By then Jahangir had long since been one of a handful of his country's most famous people and one of the very few squash players whose name is recognised outside the sport. It led to him receiving an honorary Doctorate of Philosophy from London Metropolitan University and being named by Time Magazine as one of Asia's Heroes of the last 60 years.

Jansher Khan
Jansher Khan, who won the World Open a record eight times, and the British Open six times, was one of the very best and perhaps

the most adaptable player of all time. To prosper just as much after the introduction of a two-inch lower 17-inch tin and point-per-rally scoring, which altered tactics and shortened matches in the late 1980's, he willingly evolved from a very physical style of play which had been so well suited to traditional forms of squash.

Tall and very slim, his uniquely light-footed movement and formidable stamina made him, even at an early stage, almost unbeatable. However when the parameters of professional squash changed Jansher rapidly supplemented his repertoire with a better short game and brilliant variations of strategy and pace, between rallies and within them.

He was a sensation when he burst on the scene because he dominated a Jahangir Khan who was still not far below the standard which attracted such superlative accolades for so long. Jansher was apparently only 18 years old when he beat Jahangir for the first time, at the Hong Kong Open in 1987; even more surprisingly he won their next eight encounters. One was a semi-final in the 1987 World Open, which led to his first world title, when he beat Chris Dittmar of Australia in the final.

Jansher went on to win 99 professional titles and to become the world number one for the best part of ten years, a total which is a record.

He could have won more. He was only 27 when he captured his last World Open title and not quite 28 when he won his last British Open. But by 1996 he was starting to suffer knee trouble, and the following year his movement was clearly affected. Though it was three more years before he officially retired, he was never as good again.

More people might have celebrated Jansher as the greatest, but for a controversial private life which occasionally spilled into the professional arena, and an indifferent presence which suffered by comparison with the aura exuded by Jahangir.

Peter Nicol

Although Nicol only won one World Open too, and only two British Opens at a time when the old tournament was beginning to struggle, altogether he collected 52 titles. These helped make him world number one for fully 60 months, and for 24 consecutively.

He also became the first British player to hold the world number one ranking (there were no rankings in Barrington's day) and won two very different-feeling Commonwealth Games singles gold medals, one for Scotland and one for England. His first British Open triumph, in which he beat Jansher Khan in the 1998 final, was dedicated to his German mother who died when he was 14. When his World Open title triumph came the following year he caused a majority of the 5,000 crowd to walk out, because his victory in a final in front of the Giza pyramids came against the home hero, Ahmed Barada.

Nicol's style was characterised by great movement, clever containment, excellent focus, immense tenacity, and a good brain, which helped make him excellent at finding a way to win when it seemed difficult. These were reasons why he remained at the top for so long, though another important one was his controversial change from representing Scotland to England.

Crucially this enhanced the quality of the sports science back-up after 2001, thanks to England's well-funded performance programme. It aided his fitness, his psychology, his recovery time, and his on-tour coaching. It also brought him a great deal of anguish.

There were those north of the border who resented what they saw as a betrayal, and a few expressed it in threatening terms. After winning a Commonwealth Games singles gold medal for Scotland in Kuala Lumpur in 1998, Nicol was only able to win only a silver for England in Manchester in 2002, and the tense atmosphere in which he operated may have been a factor in the defeat. Next time, in Melbourne, thousands of miles from disputes about British identity, he won gold for England.

Jonathon Power

The man who denied Nicol in the emotionally loaded circumstances at Manchester was Jonathon Power, an extrovert and unpredictably gifted Canadian, whose personality and playing style were huge contrasts with the Briton's modesty and discipline. They also enabled the two men to complement each other excellently, and made for a wonderful rivalry which brought a lively sense of theatre into squash.

Power become the first North American to become world number one, winning 36 tour titles which included a World Open and a British Open, and he returned to the top ranking fully four-and-a-half years later. It was longest gap of any repeating number one.

Given his unpromising early years, this is remarkable. There is a story about a cigarette packet falling from Power's top pocket once when he bent down in the warming up area of a tournament. It was seen by Jansher Khan who rendered an expression of disbelief. Even more did he display this emotion when four years later Power beat him.

Power had evolved from a good but variable player into an exceptional one partly by overcoming some of his personal demons, thus reducing the instability in some of his performances. Sita Schumann, his girl-friend, and Ali Al Fardan, one of the Middle East's most prominent jewellers, are both credited with roles in this.

Al Fardan was also a sponsor at the Qatar Open, and told him that if he first beat Jansher and then won the tournament he could have any ring in his store. Power duly did, and Schumann received the ring as a symbol of their engagement. Reportedly she helped him relinquish bad habits and encouraged a belief that he could be world champion.

Power became one of the game's most exciting shot-makers, developing a penchant for deception to foot-twisting levels. He was a favourite with many spectators because of his very evident emotion, and a pantomime villain with others because of his over-wrought exchanges with referees.

Although his top level successes, with only one World Open and one British Open title, were perhaps limited, Power's exhilarating style and voluble personality attracted more publicity for squash than any player of his time. In the process it helped fuel a North American boom which accelerated early in the 21st century.

David Palmer

The tall Australian was nicknamed The Marine, initially perhaps because of an erect bearing and a challenging demeanour, but eventually because he developed into one of the most remarkable fighters of all. David Palmer won four British Opens, one from match point down and one from two games down, and two World Opens, both from match point down. The second, in 2006 in front of the Giza pyramids, was arguably the most exciting world final ever, in which Palmer once again went two games down. This was against the unfortunate Gregory Gaultier of France who was denied five match points altogether.

Palmer was helped during all these crises by a superbly well-grooved orthodox style, by excellent balance during shot preparation, and by dominating volleying. He also had a capacity to strike the ball very hard, and his physical condition had become famous. In 2009 Palmer was approached by Wallabies coach Robbie Deans to help increase the rugby squad's fitness.

Despite his successes Palmer did not break through till late, at the age of 25. Given the hurdles placed in his way this was not surprising. Like all Australians he had to travel hundreds of thousands of miles to pursue a squash career, but a more unfortunate situation was that his early coach, Joe Shaw, was at odds with the head coach at the Australian Institute of Sport, Geoff Hunt, and Palmer was made to choose between them. He would have liked to work with both, but the dispute ended hopes of funding from his home country.

Statistics are sometimes said to lie, but for Palmer they are eloquent. Look at the scores of three of the six major finals he won.

Against Chris Walker of England in the 2001 British Open it was 12–15, 13–15, 15–2, 15–9, 15–5. Against John White of Australia in the 2002 World Open it was 13–15, 12–15, 15–6, 15–14, 15–11. And against Gregory Gaultier of France in the 2006 World Open it was 9–11, 9–11, 11–9, 16-14, 11–2. Each time Palmer was two games down. Each time it summoned deep survival instincts.

In a fourth major final, the 2008 British Open at Liverpool, Palmer's winning margin was just as close: 11–9, 11–9, 8–11, 6–11, 13–11, against James Willstrop of England. Twice in the last few rallies one shot was all that stood between the Marine and defeat.

Amr Shabana

Amr Shabana has often been described as the best player of the 21st century so far, and is probably the finest representative of the modern, faster, more creative, and slightly shorter version of the professional game. With its much larger synthetic rackets, sharper and faster physical demands, and much more varied tactics, modern squash makes results less predictable and champions less sure of their supremacy.

Despite these uncertainties Shabana became World Open champion four times and, after reaching world number one in 2006, stayed there for 33 months. He also remained a top level challenger for well over a decade, eventually becoming the oldest professional to capture a World Series title when winning the Tournament of Champions in New York at the age of 34 early in 2014.

Amidst these successes Shabana became the first Egyptian to win the World Open title and the first Egyptian to become world number one. His longevity, his exceptional skill, a soulful-eyed presence, and an unusual personality combining liveliness with thoughtfulness, made him one of the most popular players of all.

Curiously though he has never won the British Open, the yardstick by which early Egyptian greats such as Amr Bey, Mahmoud Karim, and Abdelfattah Aboutaleb measured themselves.

Shabana lasted so well because his early style, mixing wristy disguises, the deftest of touches, and instinctive changes of pace and direction, evolved into something more economical. Straighter, more traditional line-and-length driving acquired a greater role. A wonderful range of shots were reined in as he has become older and more cerebral.

His breakthrough came in 2003 when, as only the ninth seed, he won the World Open in Lahore, beating title-holder David Palmer in a five-game quarter-final, the Egyptian number one Karim Darwish in four, and then Thierry Lincou, the Frenchman who had made sure of becoming world number one the night before, in a very surprising four-game final.

Shabana's second world title came on the Hong Kong waterfront in 2005 when he overcame Palmer in straight games; his third arrived on a slippery glass-floored court in Bermuda In 2007 when he tirelessly beat Gaultier in three straight with his fifth title in as many weeks.

The fourth, in 2009, saw him upset the titleholder, Ramy Ashour, his younger and by now more brilliant compatriot, in straight games. It was a masterly display of control, accuracy, and patience in another final played on an open air court, set spectacularly on the shores of the Arabian Gulf in Kuwait.

By then the expressive genius had become the understated maestro.

Nick Matthew

Nick Matthew's list of successes are stunning, yet a persistently artisan image has taken a long time to catch up with his history-making roll of honour. People found it hard to comprehend that he had become as outstanding as he has.

Matthew is the only Englishman to have won three British Open titles. Then, after becoming the first Englishman to win the World Open title, he won three of those as well. That alone would surely have been enough to make him a squash legend.

But there was more. Matthew became three times a member of English world title winning teams too, and the first England-born player ever to become world number one. He was also within weeks of becoming the oldest male world champion.

This last achievement offered a clue to reason for the image-lag. Matthew was almost 30 before he topped the world rankings, past 30 before he became world champion, and well past 34 when he won the world title back.

Yet at the age of 25 he had won nothing major, and had such evident faults in his swing that critics found it hard to think that he would. But people reckoned without a special honesty to acknowledge faults and a tough-minded ability to remedy them, even at a time in his career when usually players find that impossible.

"He is unique in being able to remodel his game at such a stage," said his coach David Pearson, to whom Matthew gives much of the credit. "He accepted that unless he got his technique around acceptable areas he was never going to be a world class player. And it took him years to do it."

After he had done it, Matthew welded his remodelled stroke production to the exceptional lateral movement which facilitated his fine volleying skills. He moved quickly, took the ball early, and lasted the pace well. When a shrewdness at peaking was allied to a temperament that was sturdy under pressure, he defeated everyone—including the pundits.

Ramy Ashour

Although at the time of writing Ramy Ashour had won two World Open titles and become the first Egyptian in almost 50 years to win the British Open, it is arguable these are not his greatest achievements.

Ashour is the modern game's most charismatic personality, both on and off the court, and perhaps its most popular. He is also one of the most brilliant, albeit unorthodox, players of all time, often appearing magically to strike the ball into unexpected places, and inventing shots others would neither consider nor be able to play.

Ashour's 2012 campaign was his most successful; he became the first player to make the final of every tournament in which he competed since the Pakistani legend Jansher Khan in the mid-90's.

But 2013 was almost as good, for Ashour extended an unbeaten run to 49 matches, eventually topping the rankings with the highest points average ever recorded.

Because of all that, but perhaps too because Ashour rattles out passionate, adrenaline-fuelled comments at more than 300 words a minute—and in a foreign language, English—the BBC was moved to run a website piece asking if Ashour was the world's greatest racket sports player.

It reached no conclusion, perhaps wisely, but one of his rivals, James Willstrop, had few doubts. The Englishman wrote in his book Shot and a Ghost that Ashour "is undoubtedly one of the greatest sportsmen on the planet—certainly the most talented holding a racket in the modern generation."

The most significant blemish in his game was an early lack of sports science to help prevent injuries coming from his explosive movement. They have become career-threateningly frequent.

Ashour's winning sequence of 2013 was halted only by yet another hamstring-related injury which caused his retirement in the World Open semi-final in November. He thus relinquished his title, but not his desire and ambition. "I will come back again," he said. "I will find a way." Few would bet against it. Fewer would want to.

Heather McKay

Heather McKay may well be Australia's greatest ever sportswoman, as well as the greatest female squash player of all time, even though she competed before squash became professional and before an organised women's tour began. McKay was absolutely phenomenal. Not only did she win 16 consecutive British Open titles between 1962 and 1977, not only did she become the oldest champion by far when at the age of 39 she captured the inaugural women's World Open title in 1979, and not only did she remain undefeated during all that time, but she demolished almost all her opponents for just a handful of points.

After winning her first British Open, she never lost so much as a game, let alone a match in what was then the world's top tournament, and she remained unbeaten in everything thereafter. She only ever lost two matches, which were at the beginning of her career.

McKay hit so hard on both wings, despite an unorthodox backhand grip, and covered the court so rapidly, that she needed to spar with high quality male players—Torsam Khan, a top ten Pakistani, being one of them.

Moreover we know from one or two of her wins late in her career that she was emphatically beating opponents who were on a par with better players in the early part of the professional era.

McKay would surely have won even more British Open titles, had she not said goodbye to the tournament while still far and away the best player in 1977, four years before leaving competitive squash altogether to make a living coaching in Toronto.

McKay earned so many awards. Among them were being made a Member of the Order of the British Empire (MBE) in 1969, being made a Member of the Order of Australia in 1979, her induction into the Sport Australia Hall of Fame in 1985, and being awarded the Australian Sports Medal in 2000.

The Hitchhikers Guide to the Galaxy (earth edition) says she is the most peerless sportswoman on the planet. It sounds like an authoritative source.

Susan Devoy

Susan Devoy has been arguably the best woman player of the professional era. She won the British Open eight times when it was still regarded as the world's most important tournament. Although this impressive total is still far short of those achieved by Heather McKay and by Janet Morgan in the 50's, 60's, and 70's, theirs occurred before there was a group of full-time professionals to compete against.

Devoy won only four World Open titles, between 1985 and 1992. This though this was a phase when the women's World Open was held only biennially, preventing her tally from comparing favourably with later greats like Michelle Martin, Sarah Fitz-gerald, and Nicol David.

She was nevertheless extremely dominant during that period. Although relatively small she often appeared bigger than she was because her bouncing energy established such a formidable presence in mid-court.

The extraordinary New Zealander had six brothers and no sisters which is possibly relevant to the fact that she hit much harder than most other women, that she was unafraid to volley, and exuded a mood of aggression which could be intimidating. This sometimes extended to her relationship with the British media, some of whom, she felt, failed to give her the credit she was due.

But her feistiness paid off. From April 1984 to January 1992 she was world number one except for a brief blip early in 1988 which occurred after she made a charity walk the length of New Zealand.

By 1992, the year of her unexpected retirement, at the age of only 28, Devoy held the Australian, British, French, Hong Kong, Irish, New Zealand, Scottish, Swedish and World Open titles.

There were other stunning lists. She had already become New Zealand Sports Person of the year (1985), and a Member of the

Order of the British Empire (1986), and she was soon to become a Commander of the Order of the British Empire (1993), and a Dame Companion of the New Zealand Order of Merit (1998) when she became the youngest New Zealander since Sir Edmund Hilary in 1953 to receive a knighthood or its equivalent.

Since then she has become a forceful and occasionally controversial figure in New Zealand public life. And has four sons and no daughters.

Sarah Fitz-Gerald

Sarah Fitz-Gerald won five World Open and two British Open titles and might have won more had she continued a little longer, for she was still the world's best player when she retired in 2003 after 14 years of competition.

She might have won more too had she capitalised more on the finest volleying game the women's tour has seen. This slight shortcoming may have manifested itself because at times Fitz-Gerald lacked self-confidence.

She was three times beaten in British Open finals and once in a World Open final by Michelle Martin, an Australian compatriot who was an outstanding but not obviously better player. Fitz-Gerald's demeanour could have a self-deprecating feel. Perhaps it hindered her, but it was also this which helped make her special.

Fitz-Gerald was very popular not only because her slim frame could deliver pulverising blows to a squash ball but because she gave an impression that she thought herself no better than the rest of us. In fact she was.

Fitz-Gerald spent 50 months as world number one and was a marvellous ambassador for the sport for almost a decade as president of the Women's International Squash Players Association. She also showed that there were times when she could deal well with the multiple pressures, notably when she won the most exciting women's world final of all, at Stuttgart in 1998. Fitz-Gerald saved an amazing seven match points against Martin, recovering from 2-8 in the fifth game to triumph by 10–8, 9–7, 2–9, 3–9, 10–9.

Altogether Fitz-Gerald won 65 titles, only a handful fewer—at the time of writing—than Nicol David, whom she later coached, selflessly helping the Malaysian to surpass her own achievement of five World Open titles, at that time a record.

A year after retirement Fitz-Gerald was made a Member of the Order of Australia for her achievements and services to women's squash, and was inducted into the Sport Australia Hall of Fame six years later. It did not feel before time.

Michelle Martin

Michelle Martin, who won six British Opens and three World Opens, emerged as one of the squash greats quite unexpectedly near the turn of the millennium, having almost quit in 1990 because of what she regarded as insufficient progress. Two years later, having been becalmed on the edge of the top six, she made a dramatic push to become number one because Susan Devoy retired. It offered the prospect of better endorsements and of a life on tour, which was sometimes tough and rarely flush with money, which was suddenly a much more attractive proposition.

And what a push! After it was all over the once little known Martin had been inducted into the Australian Squash Hall of Fame, then upgraded to Legend status, before being awarded a Medal of the Order of Australia, and inducted into the World Squash Hall of Fame.

This transformation began after she appointed as her coach her uncle, Lionel Robberds, a QC in Sydney and a former cox who once competed at Henley Regatta. He helped her focus more intently, work harder, lose a lot of weight, and move better. Within weeks she became the tour's most successful player. She had already been one of the most skilful.

Michelle was awash with ability, as were most of the Martin family. Her parents built the Engadine squash centre below their family home in Sydney; she had one elder brother, Rodney Martin, who had already won the World Open, having beaten Jahangir Khan, Jansher Khan, and Chris Dittmar in a unique sequence; she had another, Brett Martin, a top five player who possibly had more talent than of any of them. It was a family almost as remarkable as the Khans of Pakistan.

Robberds' influence was considerable. Michelle Martin became world number one in 1993, held on to it for 44 months until 1996 against the challenges of Fitz-Gerald and Cassie Jackman—whom some had thought was Devoy's heir apparent—and won it back again from in both 1998 and 1999. By then Rodney had become her coach.

Martin also attracted a lot of publicity by wearing a two-piece Lycra body suit on court, but she departed as suddenly as she arrived. At the end of 1999 she announced that she had achieved all her goals, and retired. She was surprising till the end.

Nicol David

Nicol David, who had seemed diligent and worthy but discrete and self-effacing until the rat-a-tat retirements of Sarah Fitz-Gerald, Carol Owens and Cassie (Jackman) Campion, rapidly became the highest profile squash player of all time after 2005. It appeared to take the unassuming Malaysian by surprise, but given that she took her chance so well the accolade was inescapable.

David was the first Asian woman to reach the top. She was a world-beater from an ambitiously emerging nation. And she was a fascinating cultural cosmopolitan—a Christian in a Muslim country, with a Chinese mother and an Indian father, as well as academically gifted, artistically talented, and very athletic.

Eventually she broke so many records that she became an icon for a nation, for a continent, and for women. The ensuing demands on her time, energy, and emotions, and the constant pressure to maintain impeccably high standards have surely been greater than upon any other player in the game's history.

By bearing it with such commitment and grace David generated countless admirers in other regions of the world too. The uninitiated could never guess, just from speaking to her, that she had broken all professional records.

By the middle of 2014 she had won a record seven world titles and was extending her record tenure as world number one towards 100 consecutive months. She was also approaching a record 80 titles and a record 100 finals.

Her success has been based on outstanding movement and speed—especially into the counter-drop—and an ability to improve, both technically and tactically. She achieved this at her training base in Amsterdam, where she re-located to be nearer her coach Liz Irving and better sparring partners. It also offered relief from the relentless attention back home.

There she has become, the Malaysian prime minister said, more famous than he is. She has the Order of Merit, the first recipient of a top civic award established back in 1975. She has the title Datuk— perhaps an equivalent to being made a Dame in the UK—she has a stadium named after her, and she is a Goodwill Ambassador for her country.

The expectations are immense. But she does not wish to relinquish them any time soon. She aims to compete full time, she said, at least till she is 35. If possible she will continue until squash makes its debut in the Olympics.

Part Four

THE RULES
(Rules of the Game are reprinted courtesy of WSF)

Squash — Singles Rules
The definition of words in italics may be found in Appendix 1.

Introduction
Squash is played in a confined space, often at a high speed. Two principles are essential for orderly play:
Safety: Players must always place safety first and not take any action that could endanger the opponent.
Fair play: Players must respect the rights of the opponent and play with honesty.

1   THE GAME

    1.1   Singles Squash is played in a court between two players, each holding a racket to strike the ball. The court, ball, and racket must meet WSF specifications (see Appendices 7, 8 and 9).

    1.2   Each rally starts with a serve, and the players then return the ball alternately until the rally ends (see Rule 6: The Play).

    1.3   Play must be continuous as far as is practical.

2   SCORING

    2.1   The winner of a rally scores 1 point and serves to begin the next rally.

    2.2   Each game is played to 11 points, except that if the score reaches 10-all, the game continues until one player leads by 2 points.

    2.3   A match is normally the best of 5 games, but may be the best of 3 games.

    2.4   Alternative scoring systems are described in Appendix 3.

3   OFFICIALS

    3.1   A match should normally be officiated by a Marker and a Referee, both of whom must keep a record of the score, which player is serving, and the correct box for service.

    3.2   If there is only one Official, that Official is both the Marker and the Referee. A player may *appeal* any call or lack of call made by that Official as Marker to that same Official as the Referee.

3.3 The correct position for the Officials is seated at the centre of the back wall, as close to that wall as possible and just above the out-line.

3.4 An alternative Officiating System called the 3-Referee System is described in Appendix 4.

3.5 When addressing players, Officials must use the family name, where possible.

3.6 **The Marker:**

3.6.1 must announce the match, introduce each game, and announce the result of each game and of the match (see Appendix 2);

3.6.2 must call *"fault," "down," "out," "not up"* or "stop", as appropriate;

3.6.3 must make no call, if unsure about a serve or return;

3.6.4 must call the score without delay at the end of a rally, with the server's score first, preceded by *"hand" out* when there is a change of server;

3.6.5 must repeat the Referee's decision after a player's request for a let, and then call the score;

3.6.6 must wait for the Referee's decision after a player's *appeal* against a Marker's call or lack of a call, and then call the score;

3.6.7 must call "Game Ball" when a player needs 1 point to win a game, or "Match Ball" when a player needs 1 point to win the match;

3.6.8 must call "10-all: a player must win by 2 points" when the score reaches 10-all for the first time in a match.

3.7 **The Referee**, whose decision is final:

3.7.1 must postpone the match if the court is not satisfactory for play; or suspend play if the match is already in progress, and when the match resumes later, allow the score to stand;

3.7.2 must allow a let if through no fault of either player a change of court conditions affects a rally;

3.7.3 may award the match to a player whose opponent is not on court ready to play within the time stated in the competition rules;

3.7.4 must rule on all matters, including all requests for a let and all *appeals* against a Marker's call or lack of a call;

3.7.5 must rule immediately if disagreeing with the Marker's call or lack of a call, stopping play if necessary;

3.7.6	must correct the score immediately if the Marker announces the score incorrectly, stopping play if necessary;
3.7.7	must enforce all the Rules relating to time, announcing "15 seconds," "Halftime" and "Time," as appropriate;

Note: It is the players' responsibility to be close enough to hear these announcements.

3.7.8	must make the appropriate decision if the ball hits either player (see Rule 9: Ball Hitting A Player);
3.7.9	may allow a let if unable to decide an *appeal* against a Marker's call or lack of call;
3.7.10	must ask the player for clarification if uncertain about the reason for a request for a let or an *appeal;*
3.7.11	may give an explanation for a decision;
3.7.12	must announce all decisions in a voice loud enough to be heard by the players, the Marker and the spectators;
3.7.13	must apply Rule 15 (Conduct) if a player's conduct is unacceptable;
3.7.14	must suspend play if the behaviour of any person, other than a player, is disruptive or offensive, until the behaviour has ceased, or until the offending person has left the court area.

4 THE WARM-UP

4.1 At the start of a match the players go on court together to warm up the ball for a maximum of 5 minutes. After 2½ minutes the players must change sides, unless they have already done so.

4.2 The players must have equal opportunities to strike the ball. A player retaining control of the ball for an unreasonable time is warming up unfairly and Rule 15 (Conduct) must be applied.

5 THE SERVE

5.1 The player who wins the spin of a racket serves first.

5.2 At the beginning of each game and after each change of server, the server chooses from which service-box to serve. While retaining the serve, the server must serve from alternate boxes.

5.3 If a rally ends in a let, the server must serve again from the same box.

5.4 If the server moves to the wrong box to serve, or if either player is unsure of the correct box, the Marker must inform the players which is the correct box.

5.5 If there is any dispute about the correct box, the Referee must rule.

5.6 After the Marker has called the score, both players must resume play without unnecessary delay. However, the server must not serve before the receiver is ready.

5.7 A serve is good, if:

    5.7.1 the server drops or throws the ball from a hand or racket and strikes it *correctly* on a first or *further attempt* before it touches anything else; and

    5.7.2 at the time the server strikes the ball, one foot is in contact with the floor inside the service-box with no part of that foot touching any boundary of that box; and

    5.7.3 the ball is struck directly to the front wall, hitting it between the service-line and the out-line, but does not hit the front and side walls at the same time; and

    5.7.4 the ball, unless volleyed by the receiver, bounces for the first time in the opposite *quarter-court* without touching any line; and

    5.7.5 the ball is not served *out.*

5.8 A serve that does not comply with Rule 5.7 is a fault and the receiver wins the rally.

Note: A serve that hits the service-line, or the short-line, or the half-court line, or any line bounding the top of the court, is a fault.

5.9 If the server drops or throws the ball, but makes no *attempt* to strike it, this is not a serve, and the server may start again.

5.10 A let is allowed if the receiver is not ready to return the serve and does not *attempt* to do so. However, if that serve is a fault, the server loses the rally.

5.11 If the server serves from the wrong service-box, and the server wins the rally, the rally stands and the server then serves from the alternate box.

5.12 The server must not serve until the score has been called by the Marker, who must do so without delay. In such an event, the Referee must stop play and instruct the server to wait until the score has been called.

6 THE PLAY

6.1 If the serve is good, play continues as long as each return is good, or until a player requests a let or makes an *appeal,* or one of the Officials makes a call, or the ball hits either player or their clothing or the non-striker's racket.

6.2 A return is good if the ball:

6.2.1   is struck *correctly* before it has bounced twice on the floor; and

6.2.2   without hitting either player, or their clothing or racket, hits the front wall, either directly or after hitting any other wall(s), above the tin and below the out-line, without having first bounced on the floor; and

6.2.3   rebounds from the front wall without touching the tin; and

6.2.4   is not *out*.

7 INTERVALS

7.1 A maximum of 90 seconds is permitted between the end of the warm-up and the start of play, and between each game.

7.2 Players must be ready to resume play at the end of any interval, but play may resume earlier if both agree.

7.3 A maximum of 90 seconds is permitted to change damaged equipment. This includes glasses, protective eye-wear or a dislodged contact lens. The player must complete the change as quickly as possible, or Rule 15 (Conduct) must be applied.

7.4 Intervals in the case of injury or bleeding are specified in Rule 14 (Injury).

7.5 During any interval either player may strike the ball.

8 INTERFERENCE

8.1 After completing a reasonable follow-through, a player must make every effort to clear, so that when the ball rebounds from the front wall the opponent has:

8.1.1   a *fair view* of the ball on its rebound from the front wall; and

8.1.2   unobstructed direct access to the ball; and

8.1.3   the space to make a reasonable swing at the ball; and

8.1.4   the freedom to strike the ball to any part of the entire front wall.

Interference occurs when the player does not provide the opponent with all of these requirements.

8.2 A striker who believes that interference has occurred may stop and request a let, preferably by saying "Let, please." That request must be made without undue delay. Notes:

- Before accepting any form of request the Referee must be satisfied that the player is actually requesting a let.
- A request for a let includes a request for a stroke.

- Normally, only the striker may request a let for interference. However, if the nonstriker requests a let for lack of access before the ball has reached the front wall, that request may be considered, even though that player is not yet the striker.

8.3 The Referee, if uncertain about the reason for a request, must ask the player for an explanation.

8.4 The Referee may allow a let or award a stroke without a request having been made, stopping play if necessary, especially for reasons of safety.

8.5 If the striker strikes the ball and the opponent then requests a let, but then the ball goes *down* or *out*, the opponent wins the rally.

8.6 General

The following provisions apply to all forms of interference:

8.6.1   if there was neither interference nor reasonable fear of injury, no let is allowed;

8.6.2   if there was interference but the striker would not have been able to make a *good return,* no let is allowed;

8.6.3   if the striker continued play beyond the interference and then requested a let, no let is allowed;

8.6.4   if there was interference, but it did not prevent the striker from seeing and getting to the ball to make a *good return,* this is minimal interference and no let is allowed;

8.6.5   if the striker would have been able to make a *good return* but the opponent was not making every effort to avoid the interference, a stroke is awarded to the striker;

8.6.6   if there was interference that the opponent was making every effort to avoid and the striker would have been able to make a *good return,* a let is allowed;

8.6.7   if there was interference and the striker would have made a *winning return,* a stroke is awarded to the striker.

In addition to Rule 8.6, the following provisions apply to specific situations.

8.7 Fair View

Fair View means enough time to view the ball and prepare to strike it as it returns from the front wall.

8.7.1   If the striker requests a let for lack of fair view of the ball on its return from the front wall, the provisions of 8.6 apply.

8.8 Direct Access

If the striker requests a let for lack of direct access to the ball, then:

8.8.1   if there was interference but the striker did not make every effort to get to and play the ball, no let is allowed;

Note:

Every effort to get to and play the ball should not include contact with the opponent. If any contact that could have been avoided is made, Rule 15 (Conduct) must be applied.

8.8.2   if the striker had direct access but instead took an indirect path to the ball and then requested a let for interference, no let is allowed, unless Rule 8.8.3 applies;

8.8.3   if the striker was *wrong-footed,* but showed the ability to recover and make a *good return,* and then encountered interference, a let is allowed, unless the striker would have made a *winning return,* in which case a stroke is awarded to the striker.

8.9 Racket Swing

A reasonable swing comprises a reasonable backswing, a strike at the ball and a reasonable follow-through. The striker's backswing and follow-through are reasonable as long as they do not extend more than is necessary.

If the striker requests a let for interference to the swing, then:

8.9.1   if the swing was **affected** by slight contact with the opponent who was making every effort to avoid the interference a let is allowed, unless the striker would have made a *winning return,* in which case a stroke is awarded to the striker;

8.9.2   if the swing was **prevented** by contact with the opponent, a stroke is awarded to the striker, even if the opponent was making every effort to avoid the interference.

8.10 Excessive Swing

8.10.1   If the striker caused the interference by using an excessive swing, no let is allowed.

8.10.2   If there was interference but the striker exaggerated the swing in attempting to earn a stroke, a let is allowed.

8.10.3   The striker's excessive swing can contribute to interference for the opponent when it becomes the latter's turn to play the ball, in which case the opponent may request a let.

8.11 Freedom to strike the ball to any part of the entire front wall

If the striker refrains from striking the ball because of front-wall interference, and requests a let, then:

8.11.1 if there was interference and the ball would have hit the non-striker on a direct path to the front wall, a stroke is awarded to the striker, unless the striker had *turned* or was making a *further attempt,* in which case a let is allowed;

8.11.2 if the ball would first have hit the non-striker and then a side wall before reaching the front wall, a let is allowed, unless the return would have been a *winning return,* in which case a stroke is awarded to the striker; or

8.11.3 if the ball would first have hit a side wall and then the non-striker before reaching the front wall, a let is allowed unless the return would have been a *winning return,* in which case a stroke is awarded to the striker.

8.12 Further Attempt.

If the striker requests a let for interference while making a *further attempt* to strike the ball, and could have made a *good return,* then:

8.12.1 if the non-striker had no time to avoid the interference, a let is allowed.

8.13 Turning

Turning is the action of the player who strikes, or is in a position to strike, the ball to the right of the body after the ball has passed behind it to the left or vice versa, whether the player physically turns or not.

If the striker encounters interference while *turning*, and could have made a *good return*, then:

8.13.1 if the swing was prevented, even though the opponent was making every effort to avoid the interference, a stroke is awarded to the striker;

8.13.2 if the non-striker had no time to avoid the interference, a let is allowed;

8.13.3 if the striker could have struck the ball without *turning,* but turned in order to create an opportunity to request a let, no let is allowed.

8.13.4 When the striker turns, the Referee must always consider whether the action was dangerous and rule accordingly.

9 BALL HITTING A PLAYER

9.1 If the ball, on its way **to the front wall,** hits the non-striker or the non-striker's racket or clothing, play must stop; then:

9.1.1   if the return would not have been good, the non-striker wins the rally;

9.1.2   if the return was going directly to the front wall, and if the striker was making a first *attempt* without having *turned,* a stroke is awarded to the striker;

9.1.3   if the ball had hit or would have hit any other wall before the front wall and the striker had not *turned,* a let is allowed, unless the return would have been a *winning return,* in which case a stroke is awarded to the striker;

9.1.4   if the striker had not *turned* but was making a *further attempt,* a let is allowed;

9.1.5   if the striker had *turned,* a stroke is awarded to the non-striker, unless the non-striker made a deliberate movement to intercept the ball, in which case, a stroke is awarded to the striker.

9.2   If the ball, on its return **from the front wall**, hits a player before bouncing twice on the floor, play must stop; then:

9.2.1   if the ball hits the **non-striker** or the non-striker's racket, before the striker has made an *attempt* to strike the ball and no interference has occurred, the striker wins the rally, unless the striker's position has caused the non-striker to be hit, in which case a let is allowed;

9.2.2   if the ball hits the **non-striker**, or the non-striker's racket, after the striker has made one or more *attempts* to strike the ball, a let is allowed, providing the striker could have made a *good return.* Otherwise, the non-striker wins the rally;

9.2.3   if the ball hits **the striker** and there is no interference, the non-striker wins the rally. If interference has occurred, Rule 8 (Interference) applies.

9.3   If the striker hits the non-striker with the ball, the Referee must consider if the action was dangerous and rule accordingly.

10   APPEALS

10.1   Either player may stop play during the rally and appeal against any lack of call by the Marker by saying "Appeal, please."

10.2   The loser of a rally may appeal against any call or lack of a call by the Marker by saying "Appeal, please."

10.3   If the Referee is uncertain which return is being appealed, the Referee must ask for clarification. If there is more than one appeal, the Referee must consider each one.

10.4 After the ball has been served, neither player may appeal anything that occurred before that serve, with the exception of a broken ball.

10.5 At the end of a game any appeal regarding the last rally must be immediate.

10.6 In response to an appeal against a Marker's call or lack of call the Referee must:

    10.6.1   if the Marker's call or lack of call was correct, allow the result of the rally to stand; or

    10.6.2   if the Marker's call was incorrect, allow a let, unless the Marker's call interrupted a *winning return* by either player, in which case award the rally to that player; or

    10.6.3   if the Marker made no call on a serve or return that was not good, award the rally to the other player; or

    10.6.4   if the Referee was uncertain whether the serve was good, allow a let; or

    10.6.5   if the Referee was uncertain whether the return was good, allow a let, unless the Marker's call interrupted a *winning return* by the other player, in which case award the rally to that player.

10.7 In all cases the Referee's decision is final.

11 THE BALL

11.1 If the ball breaks during a rally, a let is allowed for that rally.

11.2 If a player stops play to *appeal* that the ball is broken, and it is found that the ball is not broken, that player loses the rally.

11.3 If the receiver, before *attempting* to return serve, *appeals* that the ball is broken, and the ball is found to be broken, the Referee, if uncertain when it broke, must allow a let for the previous rally.

11.4 A player who wishes to *appeal* at the end of a game that the ball is broken must do so immediately and before leaving the court.

11.5 The ball must be changed if both players agree or if the Referee agrees with one player's request.

11.6 If a ball has been replaced, or if the players resume the match after a delay, the players may warm up the ball. Play resumes when both players agree or at the discretion of the Referee, whichever is sooner.

11.7 The ball must remain in the court at all times, unless the Referee permits its removal.

11.8 If the ball becomes wedged in any part of the court, a let is allowed.

11.9 A let may be allowed if the ball touches any article in the court.

11.10 No let is allowed for any unusual bounce.

12 DISTRACTION

12.1 Either player may request a let because of distraction, but must do so immediately.

12.2 If the distraction was caused by one of the players, then:

    12.2.1 if **accidental**, a let is allowed, unless a player's *winning return* was interrupted, in which case the rally is awarded to that player;

    12.2.2 if **deliberate**, Rule 15 (Conduct) must be applied.

12.3 If the distraction was not caused by one of the players, a let is allowed, unless a player's *winning return* was interrupted, in which case the rally is awarded to that player.

12.4 At some events crowd reactions during play may occur. To encourage spectator enjoyment, Rule 12.3 may be suspended, and if sudden crowd noise occurs, players will be expected to continue play and referees will not ask spectators to be quiet. However, a player who stops play and requests a let because of a loud or isolated noise from off the court may be allowed a let for distraction.

13 FALLEN OBJECT

13.1 A player who drops a racket may pick it up and play on, unless the ball touches the racket, or distraction occurs, or the Referee applies a Conduct Penalty.

13.2 A striker who drops the racket because of interference may request a let.

13.3 A non-striker who drops the racket because of contact during the striker's effort to reach the ball may request a let, and Rule 12 (Distraction) applies.

13.4 If any object, other than a player's racket, falls to the floor during a rally, play must stop; then:

    13.4.1 if the object fell from a player without any contact with the opponent, the opponent wins the rally;

    13.4.2 if the object fell from a player because of contact with the opponent, a let is allowed, unless the striker has struck a winning return, or requests a let for interference, in which case Rule 8 (Interference) is applied;

    13.4.3 if the object falls from a source other than a player, a let is allowed, unless

    13.4.4 the striker's winning return was interrupted, in which case the rally is awarded to the striker;

13.4.5   if the object was not seen until the rally ended and had no effect on the outcome of the rally, the result of the rally stands.

14 ILLNESS, INJURY AND BLEEDING

14.1 Illness

14.1.1   A player who suffers an illness that involves neither an injury nor bleeding must either continue play immediately, or concede the game in progress and take the 90-second interval between games to recover. This includes conditions such as a cramp, nausea, and breathlessness, as well as asthma. Only one game may be conceded. The player must then resume play, or concede the match.

14.1.2   If a player's vomiting or other action causes the court to become unplayable, the match is awarded to the opponent.

14.2 Injury

The Referee:

14.2.1   if not satisfied that the injury is genuine, must advise the player to decide whether to resume play immediately, or to concede the game in progress and take the 90-second interval between games and then resume play, or concede the match. Only 1 game may be conceded;

14.2.2   if satisfied that the injury is genuine, must advise both players of the category of the injury and of the time permitted for recovery. Recovery time is permitted only at the time the injury takes place;

14.2.3   if satisfied that this is a recurrence of an injury sustained earlier in the match, must advise the player to decide whether to resume play immediately or concede the game in progress and take the 90-second interval between games, or concede the match. Only 1 game may be conceded.

Note: A player who concedes a game retains any points already scored.

14.3 Categories of injury:

14.3.1   **Self-inflicted:** where the injury is the result of the player's own action. This includes a muscle tear or sprain, or a bruise resulting from a collision with a wall or falling over.

The player is permitted 3 minutes to recover and, if not then ready to resume play, must concede that game and take the 90-second interval between games for further recovery. Only 1 game may be conceded. The player must then resume play or concede the match.

14.3.2 **Contributed:** where the injury is the result of accidental action by both players.

The injured player is permitted 15 minutes to recover. This may be extended by a further 15 minutes at the discretion of the Referee. If the player is then unable to continue, the match is awarded to the opponent. The score at the conclusion of the rally in which the injury occurred, stands.

14.3.3 **Opponent-inflicted:** where the injury is caused solely by the opponent.

14.3.3.1 Where the injury is **accidentally** caused by the opponent, Rule 15 (Conduct) must be applied. The injured player is permitted 15 minutes to recover. If the player is then unable to resume play, the match is awarded to the injured player.

14.3.3.2 Where the injury is caused by the opponent's **deliberate or dangerous** play or action, if the injured player requires any time for recovery, the match is awarded to the injured player. If the injured player is able to continue without delay, Rule 15 (Conduct) must be applied.

14.4 Bleeding

14.4.1 Whenever bleeding occurs, play must stop and the player must leave the court and attend to the bleeding promptly. Reasonable time for treatment is allowed. Play may resume only after the bleeding has stopped and, where possible, the wound has been covered.

14.4.2 If the bleeding was **accidentally caused** by the opponent, then Rule 15 (Conduct) must be applied.

14.4.3 If the bleeding is the result of the opponent's **deliberate or dangerous** play or action, the match is awarded to the injured player.

14.4.4 A player who is unable to stop the bleeding within the time permitted must either concede 1 game and take the 90-second interval and then continue play, or concede the match.

14.4.5 If blood is again visible during play, no further recovery time is permitted, and the player must concede the game in progress and use the 90-second interval between games for further treatment. If the bleeding has not then stopped, the player must concede the match.

14.4.6 The court must be cleaned and bloodstained clothing replaced.

14.5 An injured player may resume play before the end of any permitted recovery-period. Both players must be given reasonable time to prepare to resume play.

14.6 It is always the injured player's decision whether or not to resume play.

15 CONDUCT

15.1 Players must comply with any tournament regulations additional to these Rules.

15.2 Players may not place any object within the court.

15.3 Players may not leave the court during a game without the permission of the Referee.

15.4 Players may not request a change of any Official.

15.5 Players must not behave in a manner that is unfair, dangerous, abusive, offensive, or in any way detrimental to the sport.

15.6 If a player's conduct is unacceptable, the Referee must penalise the player, stopping play if necessary.

Unacceptable behaviour includes, but is not limited to:

15.6.1 audible or visible obscenity;

15.6.2 verbal, physical or any other form of abuse;

15.6.3 unnecessary physical contact, which includes pushing off the opponent;

15.6.4 dangerous play, including an excessive racket swing;

15.6.5 dissent to an Official;

15.6.6 abuse of equipment or court;

15.6.7 unfair warm-up;

15.6.8 delaying play, including being late back on court;

15.6.9 deliberate distraction;

15.6.10 receiving coaching during play.

15.7 A player guilty of an offence may be given a Conduct Warning or penalised with a Conduct Stroke, a Conduct Game, or a Conduct Match, depending on the severity of the offence.

15.8 The Referee may impose more than one warning, stroke or game to a player for a subsequent similar offence, providing any such penalty may not be less severe than the previous penalty for the same offence.

15.9 A warning or a penalty may be imposed by the Referee at any time, including during the warm-up and following the conclusion of the match.

15.10 If the Referee:

15.10.1 stops play to issue a Conduct Warning, a let is allowed;

15.10.2 stops play to award a Conduct Stroke, that Conduct Stroke becomes the result of the rally;

15.10.3 awards a Conduct Stroke after a rally has finished, the result of the rally stands, and the Conduct Stroke is added to the score with no change of service-box;

15.10.4 awards a Conduct Game, that game is the one in progress or the next one if a game is not in progress. In the latter case an additional interval of 90 seconds does not apply;

15.10.5 awards a Conduct Game or a Conduct Match, the offending player retains all points or games already won;

15.11 When a Conduct Penalty has been imposed, the Referee must complete any required documentation.

APPENDIX 1—DEFINITIONS

APPEAL
: A player's request to the Referee to review a Marker's call or lack of a call, or to appeal that the ball is broken.

ATTEMPT
: Any forward movement of the racket towards the ball. A fake swing is also an attempt, but racket preparation with only a backswing and no forward movement towards the ball is not an attempt.

BOX, SERVICE-BOX
: A square area on each side of the court bounded by the short-line, a side wall and by 2 other lines, from where the server serves.

CORRECTLY
: When the ball is struck with the racket, held in the hand, not more than once, and without prolonged contact on the racket.

DOWN
: A return that hits the tin or the floor before reaching the front wall, or hits the front wall and then the tin.

FAIR VIEW
: Enough time to view the ball and prepare to strike it as it returns from the front wall.

FAULT
: A serve that is not good.

FURTHER ATTEMPT
: A subsequent attempt by the striker to serve or return a ball that is still in play, after having already made one or more attempts.

GAME
: A part of a match. A player must win 3 games to win a best of 5-game match and 2 games to win a best of 3-game match.

GOOD RETURN
: A return that is struck correctly and that travels to the front wall either directly or after hitting another wall or walls without going out, and that hits the front wall above the tin and below the out-line.

HAND OUT
: A change of server.

LET
: The result of a rally that neither player wins. The server serves again from the same box.

MATCH
: The complete contest, including the warm-up.

NOT UP
: A return that:
    a player does not strike correctly; or
    bounces more than once on the floor before being struck; or
    touches the striker or the striker's clothing.

OUT
: A return that:
    hits the wall on or above the out-line; or
    hits any fixture above the out-line; or
    hits the top edge of any wall of the court; or
    passes over a wall and out of the court; or
    passes through any fixture.

QUARTER-COURT
: One of two equal parts of the court bounded by the short-line, a side wall, the back wall and the half-court line.

RALLY
: A good serve followed by one or more alternate returns until one player fails to make a good return.

SERVICE-BOX
: See BOX, SERVICE-BOX.

STRIKER	A player is the striker from the moment the opponent's return rebounds from the front wall until the player's return hits the front wall.
TIN	The area of the front wall covering the full width of the court and extending from the floor up to and including the lowest horizontal line.
TURNING	The action of the striker who strikes, or is in a position to strike, the ball to the right of the body after the ball has passed behind it to the left or vice versa, whether the striker physically turns or not.
	Note: Shaping (preparing) to play the ball on one side and then bringing the racket across the body to strike the ball on the other side is neither turning nor making a further attempt.
WINNING RETURN	A good return that the opponent could not reach.
WRONG-FOOTED	The situation when a player, anticipating the path of the ball, moves in one direction, while the striker strikes the ball in another direction.

APPENDIX 2—OFFICIALS' CALLS

2.1 MARKER

DOWN	To indicate that a player's return hit the tin, or the floor before reaching the front wall, or hit the front wall and then the tin.
FAULT	To indicate that a serve was not good.
HAND OUT	To indicate a change of server.
NOT UP	To indicate that a return:

> was not struck correctly; or
>
> bounced more than once on the floor before being struck; or
>
> touched the striker or the striker's clothing.

OUT	To indicate that a return:

> hit the wall on or above the out-line; or
>
> hit any fixture above the out-line; or
>
> hit the top edge of any wall of the court or passed over a wall and out of the court;
>
> or passed through any fixture.

10-ALL: A PLAYER MUST WIN BY 2 POINTS

To indicate at 10-all that a player must lead by 2 points to win the game. Called only on the first occurrence in a match.

GAME BALL	To indicate that a player requires one point to win the game.
MATCH BALL	To indicate that a player requires one point to win the match.
YES, LET/ LET	To repeat the Referee's decision that a rally is to be re-played.

STROKE TO (PLAYER or TEAM)

To repeat the Referee's decision to award a stroke to a player or team.

NO LET	To repeat the Referee's decision that a request for a let is disallowed.

Examples of Marker's Calls

1. Match introduction:
    "Smith to serve, Jones to receive, best of 5 games, love-all."
2. Order of calls:
    i)   Anything affecting the score (e.g. Stroke to Brown).
    ii) The score with the server's score always called first.
    iii) Comments on the score (e.g. Game ball).
3. Calling the score:
    "Not up. Hand-out, 4–3."
    "Yes let, 3–4."
    "Stroke to Jones, 10–8, Game Ball."
    "Fault, hand-out, 8–3."
    "Not up, 10-all: a player must win by 2 points."
    "10–8, Match Ball."
    "13–12, Match Ball."

4. End of a game:
   "11–3, game to Smith. Smith leads 1 game to love."
   "11–7, game to Jones. Smith leads 2 games to 1."
   "11–8, match to Jones, 3 games to 2, 3–11, 11–7, 6–11, 11–9, 11–8."
5. Start of successive games:
   "Smith leads 1 game to love. Love-all."
   "Smith leads 2 games to 1. Jones to serve, love-all."
   "2 games all. Smith to serve, love-all."

2.2 REFEREE

FIFTEEN SECONDS	To advise that 15 seconds of a permitted interval remain.
HALF-TIME	To advise that 2½ minutes of the warm-up period have passed.
LET / PLAY A LET	To advise that a rally is to be replayed in circumstances where the wording "Yes, Let" is not appropriate (e.g. when neither player has requested a let).
NO LET	To disallow a let.
STROKE TO *(player or team)*	To advise that a stroke is being awarded.
TIME	To indicate that a permitted interval has elapsed.
YES, LET	To allow a let.
CONDUCT WARNING	To advise that a Conduct Warning is being issued, e.g.: "Conduct Warning Smith for delaying play."
CONDUCT STROKE	To advise that a Conduct Stroke is being awarded, e.g.: "Conduct Smith, Stroke to *(other player or team)* for delay of game."
CONDUCT GAME	To advise that a Conduct Game is being awarded, e.g.: "Conduct Jones, Game to *(other player or team)* for abuse of opponent."
CONDUCT MATCH	To advise that a Conduct Match is being awarded, e.g.: "Conduct Jones, Match to *(other player or team)* for dissent to Referee."

127

APPENDIX 3—ALTERNATIVE SCORING SYSTEMS

1.   Point-a-rally scoring to 15

Rule 2 (Scoring) is replaced by (see italics):

2.1   The winner of a rally scores 1 point and serves to begin the next rally.

2.2   *Each game is played to 15 points, except that if the score reaches 14-all, the game continues until one player leads by 2 points.*

2.3   A match is normally the best of 5 games, but may be the best of 3.

2.   Hand-in/hand-out scoring

Rule 2 (Scoring) is replaced by (see italics):

2.1   *The server, on winning a rally, scores a point; the receiver, on winning a rally, becomes the server without a change of score.*

2.2   *Each game is played to 9 points, except that if the score reaches 8-all, the receiver chooses, before the next service, to continue that game either to 9 (known as "Set 1") or to 10 (known as "Set 2"). The receiver must clearly indicate this choice to the Marker, Referee and the opponent.*

2.3   A match is normally the best of 5 games, but may be the best of 3.

APPENDIX 4—THE THREE-REFEREE SYSTEM

1. The Three-Referee System uses a Central Referee (CR) and two Side Referees (SRs) who must work together as a team. All should be the highest accredited referees available. If the 3 Officials are not of a similar standard, then the Referee of the highest standard should normally act as the CR.

2. The CR, who is also the Marker, controls the match and must consult with the SRs before the match and if necessary (and if possible) between games, to try and ensure consistency of rules application and interpretation. One of the SRs keeps score as a backup. In the event of a discrepancy the CR's score is final.

3. The two SRs should be seated behind the back wall in line with the inside line of the service box on each side, one row in front of the CR.

4. The SRs make decisions at the end of rallies—not during them—on the following matters only:

   4.1 When a player requests a let; or appeals against a call or lack of a call of down, not up, out, or fault by the CR.

   4.2 If any Referee is unsighted that Referee's decision is "Yes, Let."

   4.3 If the CR is unsure of the reason for an appeal, the CR must ask the player for clarification.

   4.4 If a SR is unsure of what is being appealed, the SR must ask the CR for clarification.

5. Only the CR decides all other matters including time-periods, conduct, injury, distraction, broken ball, fallen object, and court conditions, none of which may be appealed.

6. Every appeal must be decided by all 3 Referees, simultaneously and independently.

7. A majority decision of the 3 referees is final, unless a video referee system is in operation.

8. The decision of the 3 Referees must be announced by the CR without revealing the individual decisions.

9. In the case of 3 different decisions (Yes Let, No Let, Stroke), the final decision will be "Yes, Let."

10. Players may speak only to the CR. Dialogue must be kept to a minimum.

11. The Referees may give their decisions using (in order of preference):

    1. Electronic consoles; or
    2. Referee Decision Cards; or
    3. Hand signals.

12. If hand-signals are used:

    Yes, Let = Thumb and forefinger in the shape of an 'L'.

    Stroke = Clenched fist.

    No Let = Hand held out flat, palm downwards.

    Ball was Down/ Not Up/ Out/ Fault = Thumb Down.

    Ball was Good = Thumb Up.

APPENDIX 5—VIDEO REVIEW

May be used where the technology is available.

RULES/PROCEDURE

1. A player may request a review of an Interference decision of Let, Stroke or No Let only, but may not appeal any Marker calls. Each player has one review per game; if the original decision is overruled, the player retains the review.
2. The player must clearly and immediately ask the Central Referee (CR) for a "Video Review, please."
3. The CR then states: "Video review, please, (player's name), on the Yes, Let/No Let/Stroke decision."
4. The replays will be shown on the screens.
5. The decision of the Video Review Official, whose decision is final, will be displayed on the screens.
6. The CR then states either: "Yes, Let/No Let/Stroke decision upheld, (player's name) has no review remaining"; or "Yes, Let/No Let/Stroke decision overruled, (player's name) has 1 review remaining."
7. When the score reaches 10-all, each player will have only 1 further review available. Unused reviews may not be carried over beyond the score of 10-all or into any following games. The CR announces: "10-all, a player must win by 2 points. Each player has 1 review available."
8. If a video review is unavailable because of technical difficulties, this will not count as a review being used.

APPENDIX 6—PROTECTIVE EYEWEAR

The WSF recommends that all squash players should wear protective eyewear, manufactured to an appropriate National Standard, properly over the eyes at all times during play, including the warm-up. Current National Standards for Racket Sport Eye Protection are published by the Canadian Standards Association, the United States ASTM, Standards Australia/New Zealand and British Standards Institution. It is the responsibility of the player to ensure that the quality of the product worn is appropriate for the purpose.

Protective eyewear, meeting any of the above standards (or equivalent), is mandatory for all doubles and junior events sanctioned by the WSF.

APPENDIX 7—TECHNICAL SPECIFICATIONS

APPENDIX 7.1
DESCRIPTION AND DIMENSIONS OF A SINGLES COURT
DESCRIPTION

A squash court is a rectangular area bounded by 4 walls: the front wall, 2 side walls and the back wall. It has a level floor and a clear height above the court area.

DIMENSIONS

Length of court between playing surfaces	9750 mm
Width of court between playing surfaces	6400 mm
Diagonal	11665 mm
Height above floor to lower edge of front-wall line	570 mm
Height above floor to lower edge of back-wall line	2130 mm
Height above floor to lower edge of service-line on front wall	1780 mm
Height above floor to upper edge of tin	480 mm
Distance to nearest edge of short-line from back wall	4260 mm
Internal dimensions of service-boxes	1600 mm
Width of all lines	50 mm
Minimum clear height above the floor of the court	5640 mm

NOTES

1. The side-wall lines connect the front-wall line and the back-wall line.
2. The service-box is a square formed by the short-line, one side wall and two other lines marked on the floor.
3. The length, width and diagonal of the court are measured at a height of 1000 mm above the floor.
4. It is recommended that the front-wall line, side-wall lines, back-wall line and the top 50 mm of the tin be shaped so as to deflect any ball that strikes them.
5. The tin must not project from the front wall by more than 45 mm.
6. It is recommended that the door to the court be in the centre of the back wall.
7. The general configuration of a squash court, its dimensions and its markings are illustrated on the diagram at Appendix 7.2.

CONSTRUCTION

A squash court may be constructed from various materials providing they have suitable ball rebound characteristics and are safe for play; however, the WSF publishes a Squash Court Specification which contains recommended standards. A National or Regional Governing Body may require that the WSF standards must be met for competitive play.

APPENDIX 7.2
GENERAL CONFIGURATION OF THE INTERNATIONAL SINGLES COURT

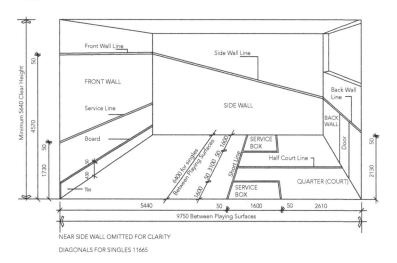

NEAR SIDE WALL OMITTED FOR CLARITY

DIAGONALS FOR SINGLES 11665

APPENDIX 8—SPECIFICATIONS OF SQUASH BALLS

1. A STANDARD DOUBLE YELLOW DOT (Competition) BALL

The following specification is the standard for a double yellow dot (Competition) ball to be used under the Rules of Squash:

Diameter (millimetres) 40.0 + or – 0.5

Weight (grams) 24.0 + or – 1.0

Stiffness (N/mm) @ 23 degrees C. 3.2 + or – 0.4

Seam Strength (N/mm) 6.0 minimum

Rebound Resilience—from 254 centimetres

   @ 23 degrees C. 12% minimum

   @ 45 degrees C. 25% – 30%

2. A STANDARD SINGLE YELLOW DOT (Club) BALL

The following specification is the standard for a single yellow dot (Club) ball to be used under the Rules of Squash:

Diameter (millimetres) 40.0 + or – 0.5

Weight (grams) 24.0 + or – 1.0

Stiffness (N/mm) @ 23 degrees C. 3.2 + or – 0.4

Seam Strength (N/mm) 6.0 minimum

Rebound Resilience—from 254 centimetres

   @ 23 degrees C. 15% minimum

   @ 45 degrees C. 30% – 35%

NOTES

1. The full procedure for testing balls to the above specifications is available from the WSF. The WSF will arrange for testing of balls under standard procedures if requested.

2. No specifications are set for faster or slower speeds of ball, which may be used by players of greater or lesser ability or in court conditions which are hotter or colder than those used to determine the Club and Competition specifications. Where faster speeds of ball are produced they may vary from the diameter and weight in the above specifications. It is recommended that balls bear a permanent colour code or marking to indicate their speed or category of usage. It is also recommended that balls for beginners and improvers conform generally to the rebound resilience figures below.

    Beginner Rebound resilience @ 23 degrees C not less than 17%

    Rebound resilience @ 45 degrees C. 36% to 38%

    Improver Rebound resilience @ 23 degrees C. not less than 15%

    Rebound resilience @ 45 degrees C. 33% to 36%

    Specifications for balls currently fulfilling these requirements can be obtained from the WSF on request.

The speed of balls may also be indicated as follows:
Super slow—Yellow Dot (Single or Double)
Slow—White Dot or Green Dot
Medium—Red Dot
Fast—Blue Dot

3. Balls which are used at World Championships or at similar standards of play must meet the above specifications for the Standard Double Dot (Competition) ball. Additional subjective testing may be carried out by the WSF with players of the identified standard to determine the suitability of the nominated ball for Championship usage.

4. Yellow dot balls of a larger diameter than 40.0 mm specified above, but which otherwise meet the specification, may be authorised for use in tournaments by the official organising body.

APPENDIX 9—DIMENSIONS OF A SQUASH RACKET

DIMENSIONS

Maximum length 686 mm
Maximum width, measured at right angles to the shaft 215 mm
Maximum length of strings 390 mm
Maximum strung area 500 sq. cm
Minimum width of any frame or any structural member (measured in plane of strings) 7 mm
Maximum depth of any frame or other structural member (measured at right angles to plane of strings) 26 mm
Minimum radius of outside curvature of frame at any point 50 mm
Minimum radius of curvature of any edge of frame or other structural member 2 mm

WEIGHT

Maximum weight 255 gm

CONSTRUCTION

a) The head of the racket is defined as that part of the racket containing or surrounding the strung area.

b) Strings and string ends must be recessed within the racket head or, in cases where such recessing is impractical because of racket material, or design, must be protected by a securely attached bumper strip.

c) The bumper strip must be made of a flexible material which cannot crease into sharp edges following abrasive contact with the floor or walls.

d) The bumper strip shall be of a white, colourless or unpigmented material. Where for cosmetic reasons a manufacturer chooses to use a coloured bumper strip, then the manufacturer shall demonstrate to the satisfaction of the WSF that this does not leave a coloured deposit on the walls or floor of the court after contact.

e) The frame of the racket shall be of a colour and/or material which will not mark the walls or floor following an impact in normal play.

f) Strings shall be gut, nylon or a substitute material, provided metal is not used.

g) Only two layers of strings shall be allowed and these shall be alternately interlaced or bonded where they cross and the string pattern shall be generally uniform and form a single plane over the racket head.

h) Any grommets, string spacers or other devices attached to any part of the racket shall be used solely to limit or prevent wear and tear or vibration and be reasonable in size and placement for such purpose. They shall not be attached to any part of the strings within the hitting area (defined as the area formed by overlapping strings).

i) There shall be no unstrung areas within the racket construction such that will allow the passage of a sphere greater than 50 mm in diameter.

j) The total racket construction including the head shall be symmetrical about the centre of the racket in a line drawn vertically through the head and shaft and when viewed face on.

k)   All changes to the racket specification will be subject to a notice period of two years before coming into force.

The WSF shall rule on the question of whether any racket or prototype complies with the above specifications, or is otherwise approved or not approved for play and will issue guidelines to assist in the interpretation of the above.

Lightning Source UK Ltd.
Milton Keynes UK
UKOW07f1839110215

246119UK00001B/1/P